THE TRUE BEGINNER'S
GUIDE
TO COMPUTER LITERACY

THE TRUE BEGINNER'S GUIDE TO COMPUTER LITERACY

DO IT YOURSELF, NO TEACHER, NO HELP NEEDED. ALL YOU NEED IS: THIS BOOK, YOU AND A COMPUTER

RETZER DORVILUS

MICROSOFT CERTIFIED SYSTEMS ENGINEER
AND MICROSOFT CERTIFIED TECHNOLOGY SPECIALIST
MCP, MCSA, MCSE and MCTS. (2008)

To order additional copies of this book, contact:
Xlibris Corporation
1-888-795-4274
www.Xlibris.com
Orders@Xlibris.com
64875

THE TRUE BEGINNER'S GUIDE
TO COMPUTER LITERACY

**JUST SIT BEFORE YOUR
COMPUTER AND OPEN YOUR
BOOK THEN FOLLOW STEP BY STEP**

About the Author

RETZER DORVILUS is a product of P.C. Professor. He has successfully completed the Microsoft requirements and recognized as MCP, MCSA, MCSE, and MCTS.

Mr. DORVILUS has a wealth of knowledge in the building and repair of computer so much so after graduating from Foley-Belsaw Institute he established his own computer store. Under the name RETZER Electronics Engineering Computer Service Center. Determining to share his knowledge, he has now written his first book entitle "TRUE BEGINNER'S GUIDE TO COMPUTER LITERACY". He has traveled extensively to Mexico, Jamaica, and Haiti, to name a few; and has taught over ten (10) years, in four (4) languages.

RETZER DORVILUS can be found either in his office typing away, at his computer, troubleshooting or researching on some special task. He likes to play table tennis, and music. In fact he is a people concept. His dream is to reach as many as he can to empower their mind by coaching, counseling or teaching.

CONTENTS AT A GLANCE

THE TRUE BEGINNER'S GUIDE TO COMPUTER LITERACY

This guide provides step-by-step instructions of how to become computer literate. Follow this guide carefully; you will be on your way of becoming computer smart. Specific tasks included in this guide are:

CONTENTS

Introduction

Chapter 1

Chapter 2

CHAPTER 3

CHAPTER 4

CHAPTER 5

CHAPTER 6

CHAPTER 7

CHAPTER 8

CHAPTER 9

DEDICATION

To Vinora for her encouragement. To VERNALEE, who played an active part and her support? To Roselene and Shaunalee who patiently wait for their dinner and wondering when will dad have a chance to go out with us? And also to Rose-Andrée. Dr. Junior Esau, Berns, Jose, Vasthie, Pauline and Ezelle.

AUTHOR'S ACKNOWLEDGMENTS

Grateful acknowledgment is expressed to VINORA for her superb innovative idea of this book being born; To ALTHEA for her time and talent in editing and informative suggestions; to my main editor VERNALEE for her masterly creative input in all phases of the production of this, my first effort at writing a computer basic guide book.

I love to lose myself in other men's minds.
When I am not walking, I am reading; I
Cannot sit and think. Books think for me.
By Charles Lamb.

CHAPTER 1

THOUGHT FROM THE AUTHOR

ATTITUDE

Attitude, to me, is more important than facts. The longer I live, the more I realize the impact of attitude. It is more important than the past, than education, than money, than circumstances, than failures, than success, than whatever people think or say or do. It is more important than appearance, giftedness or skill. It can make you succeed or disrupt your life forever. It can make or break a company, a church, and a home. The remarkable thing is we have a choice, every day regarding the attitude we will embrace for that day.

We cannot change our past. We cannot change the fact that people will act in a certain way. We cannot change the inevitable. The only thing we can do; is to play on the string we have, and that is our attitude. I am convinced that life is 10% of what happens to me, and 90% of how I react to it. And so it is with you. We are in charge of our attitude.

By Charles Swindoll

HOW TO USE THIS BOOK

Welcome to the first volume of the **"TRUE BEGINNER'S GUIDE TO COMPUTER LITERACY."** Every thing in life requires a skill, without that your labor is in vain. Especially for jobs purposes you have to have a specialized skill in order to make it. This book is not intended to prepare you for a better job; but it can help you to achieve your goal for a better position in life.

This volume covers: How to turn your computer on/off including "Vista". It also guides you through the system data so that you can be able to search for programs and be able to create users account. It also teaches the full use of the keyboard and how to manipulate the mouse. Just in this volume you will learn how to use Microsoft Word and paint and how to use all the features on the task bar "such as: File, Edit, View, Insert, Format, Tools, Table, Window and help. It also teaches you how to start or manipulate a program and how to install software on your computer and how to print and most importantly it teaches how to use your computer to take pictures of itself without the use of a camera and how to convert word file to JPEG file. It also motivates you how to become an excellent typist. You will also learn how to use your PC as CD player, navigate on the Internet, and create a Free E-mail account, also the importance of anti-virus.

Then it goes to the integrity of the computer to show the different parts that form the system and their name so that you may be familiar with them.

This book is not intended to use theoretically, but both theory and practical. As you hold a copy of this book, you need to have access to a computer as well. If you cannot afford a new one, look for a cheap one at a thrift store or a pawnshop. Make sure you have the right attitude toward your learning in order to succeed. Now you are on your way of becoming a computer smart.

PRESS ON

Nothing in the world can take the place of persistence. Talent will not; nothing is more common than unsuccessful men with talent. Genius will not; unrewarded genius is almost a proverb. Education alone will not; the world is full of educated derelicts. PERSISTENCE and DETERMINATION alone are omnipotent.

Do not allow yourself to become upset by people, places, things, or circumstances, they are powerless, your reactions is their only power.

5 P's **RULES TO OBSERVE**

PROPER PLANNING

PREVENTS POOR

PERFORMANCE

HOW TO POWER ON YOUR COMPUTER

Figure 1.1 shows the power button to turn on your computer. Gently press in the power button with your index finger and release it. Now watch the screen do not touch the keyboard nor the mouse until you see the screen like the one in figure 1.4 it also shows you how to open the CD—Rom later in the lesson you'll learn the proper way to insert your CD into the CD—Rom drive. There are different shapes and sizes of computer, do not be deceived by their look. There is only one way to power on your PC. The power button can be found either on the right side of the CD-ROM or to the left side or below the CD-ROM. Most of the power buttons are like a circle. Some computers have two buttons, one big and one small. The big one is the power button. The small one is reset button and it can be used only when there is problem on the screen, gently press the reset button and release it, the computer will restart then the screen will be cleared.

Open CD-Rom here

Press this to Power
on your PC

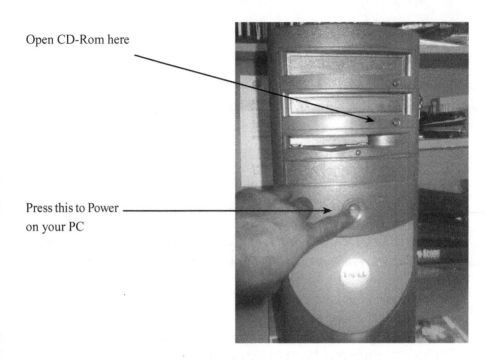

Fig.1.1

Click here to
power on your
PC

Click here to
restart your
PC

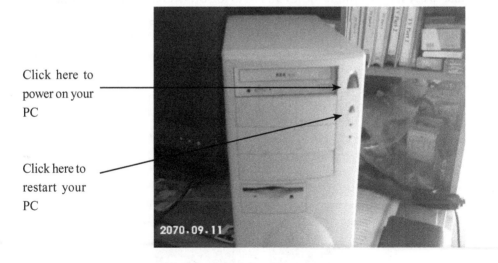

Fig. 1.2

How to turn off your Computer using

windows XP or Vista?

Do not turn off your Computer the same way you turn it on, you may damage it if you do. Make sure you finish using it for the day before you turn it off. Do not use your computer as you use your television by turning it on/off 10 to 20 times a day it's not good for your computer's health. *Now follow the procedure carefully to turn off your Computer.* Figure 1.3 put the mouse pointer on the word start, which is at the bottom left of your PC (The word PC stand for Personal Computer, so time to time you'll see the term PC instead of computer do not be confused.) Click it once and you'll see the screen appears like the one in figure 1.4 ► Two icons, one mark log off and the other one turn off. What's the difference between log off and turn off your PC? Log off (for example if you have more than one username on your PC like Patt, Yvonne and so on, Patt is presently using the computer and Yvonne comes, she would like to use it for a minute, now Patt has to log off her name so that Yvonne can log on her's and so on. Turn off is when no one is going to use it, now you can click on "turn off" and another screen will appear like the one on figure 1.5

Fig.1.3

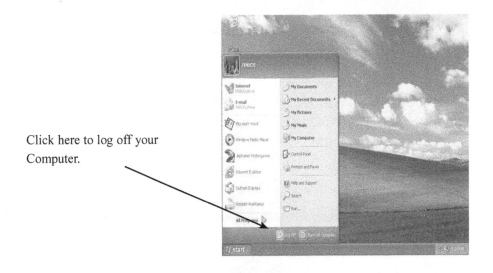

Click here to log off your
Computer.

Fig.1.4

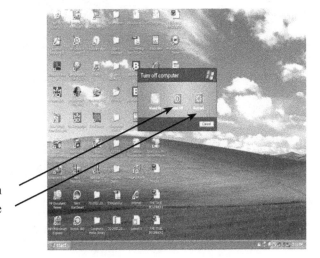

Click on the middle button
to turn off your PC/ the
right one to restart

Fig.1.5

Then position your mouse pointer on the center icon that is in red, and then click it once. Your PC will go off by itself; you don't need to do anything else. And also the monitor will automatically put in a sleeping mode until you turn the computer back on. You will notice a very small amber light like a dot beside the power button on the monitor if you

17

don't want it to stay on, simply press it down with your index finger, and release it. Then it will be completely off. Remember you don't have to power off your monitor, if you do, when power on the PC you will also have to power on the monitor.

▶ For windows vista it is slightly different. When you position your mouse pointer on the window logo that is on the bottom left corner on your screen, click it once then a screen will appear like the one on figure1.6

Make your selection here
(Shut down, log off or restart)

Fig.1.6

▶ Then move the mouse pointer to your right, position the pointer to the arrow that point to your right hand side▶ then you'll see a little window that appears in that window; there are about 7 words. Switch user, log off, lock, restart, sleep, hibernate, and shut down. Since you want to turn off click shut down. Then the system will turn off itself.

How to search for programs

Now you are ready to handle your mouse do not be afraid of it. It is not a real mouse. It will not bite you. Touch it; hold it in your hand. It is not soft as the real mouse as you can see.

First look at the screen on figure 1.3 look for the word start at the bottom left on your computer. Position the arrow ▲ on the word *start* from your monitor screen it will tell you click here to begin. Gently click on the left side of your mouse as you see on figure 1.7 Make sure your fingers do not rest on the right side of your mouse, clicking the right side will give a different command to your PC which you don't want to. Avoid it until you learn the use of it.

After you click start, another window will appear with several icons like the one on figure 1.8 you will see; internet explorer, E-mail, outlook express, windows media player, all programs, my documents, my computer, control panel, printer & faxes, help support, search, run

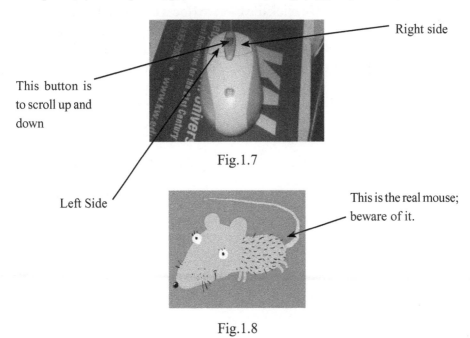

Right side

This button is to scroll up and down

Fig.1.7

Left Side

This is the real mouse; beware of it.

Fig.1.8

Understanding My Computer

Sitting on the screen of every Windows PC is a very useful tool call My Computer. At first, it may not appear to do much, but it can be used in several different ways and is certainly worth exploring.

A DATA WAREHOUSE

In simple terms, My Computer acts as a kind of warehouse, storing the most important departments, or areas, of your computer, but more than this, My Computer also acts like a doorway, allowing you to tour your PC, your folders and files, and keep tracks of your work.

Look at figure 1.9 the My Computer icon can be the third or the fifth icon to your right. Gently place the mouse pointer on My Computer icon double click it to open my computer icon. It will open like figure 2.1 this is for windows XP, double click the C drive (local disk(C:)) that can be the first one to your right. A list of programs will appear like the one on figure 2.2 this shows you everything that is stored on your PC hard drive.

Please do not delete anything from your hard drive unless you know exactly what you are doing, otherwise you may mess up your computer system. Later you'll learn how to delete or remove unwanted file or folder.

Your screen
Should look like
this one.

Fig.1.9

Local Disk (C:)

Fig.2.1

CREATING USER ACCOUNTS

Remember that your mouse is user friendly. Now hold your mouse, move the pointer to the bottom left corner of your screen put it on the word *start* click the left side on your mouse with your index finger one time. A screen will appear like the one in figure 2.2

Fig.2.2

▶ Next step move the mouse pointer to the word "settings" that is the sixth word from the bottom of your screen to the top.

▶ Second step, move the mouse pointer gently across to the word Control Panel, then click on the left hand side of your mouse once. Then the Control Panel drop box will appear like the one in the figure 2.3

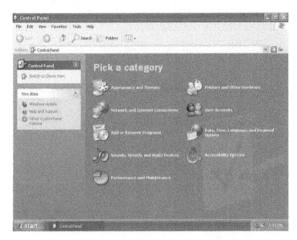

Fig.2.3

▶ Please look carefully on the Control Panel drop box. Can you see the phrase "Pick a category" there are several icons; the one you need now is this one. Figure 2.4

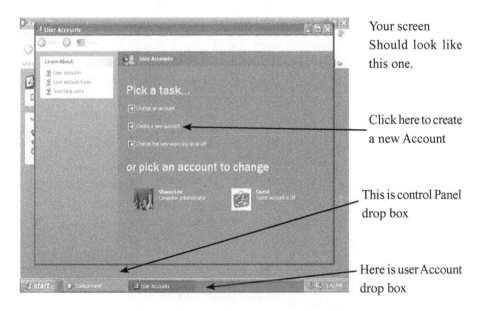

Your screen Should look like this one.

Click here to create a new Account

This is control Panel drop box

Here is user Account drop box

Fig.2.4

▶ Place the mouse pointer on the words "User Accounts" and click it one time remember to use the left side of your mouse and a next drop box will appear which is the User accounts drop box.

23

▶ Now position the mouse pointer on the second box that is "create a new account", click it one time, and watch the screen below. Figure 2.5

Type a name for the new user Account here

Fig.2.5

▶ Follow the instruction use the keyboard to type the name for the new account then click next. It will appear like the one below, figure 2.6. Click creates by clicking on the left side of your mouse.

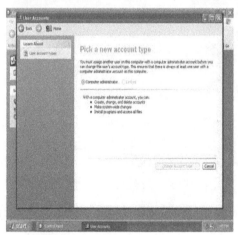

Fig.2.6

▶ If you have more than one person using the computer the choice is yours. You can create separate account for each one, just follow the same procedure.

CHANGE THE LOOK OF YOUR SCREEN

In order to change the look of your screen you first have to get to the display properties. There are many ways to get to the display properties.

▶ First, the quick way is to click the right side of your mouse like in the picture below, figure 2.7

Fig.2.7

▶ Then a drop box will appear with some icons as you can see in the figure.

▶ Then gently move the mouse pointer down to Properties. Then click on it once. The display properties drop box will appear like the one below, figure 2.8

Fig.2.8

▶ Next step, look carefully at the display properties drop box. Can you see those five (5) icons under the words Display Properties? Now use the mouse pointer, position it on the word desktop, and use your index finger to click on the left side of your mouse one time. That is it. Does your screen look like the one below? Figure 2.9. Take time to compare them.

Fig.2.9

▶ Now you can explore to find out the look for each one as you make a left click on each one once at a time and watch the changes on the screen that appears inside the properties drop box.

▶ Click on Ascent and watch the screen, next autumn and watch the screen you can continue until you see all of them. Does your screen look like the one below? Figure 3.0

Fig. 3.0

▶ After you make your selection click the word "Apply" then click "Ok" to finish.

▶ Next step let's say that I want to put my favorite picture as my desktop background. How do you do that?

▶ Very good there are three (3) ways you can use to make it possible.

▶ The first way is; if you have a printer that is "all in one". Meaning that it can print, scan/copy and fax as well. You can place your favorite picture into the scanner and press scan then it is scanned to your computer. Then click save. It will ask you *under what name would you like to save it.* Then you can type a name under which you'd like it to be saved; then click *save* for a second time.

▶ Next step go to your desktop double click the "My Computer" icon by placing your index finger on the left side of your mouse. Then a screen will appear as in figure 3.1

▶ Then double click the icon "share documents or my documents" next you'll see the name under which you saved your picture. Let's say for example you call it "my picture" double click my picture icon. Does your screen look like figure 3.2?

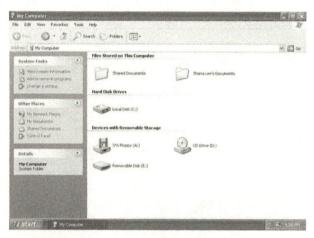

Fig.3.1

▶ Then double click on the picture. Does it look like the one below?

Fig.3.2

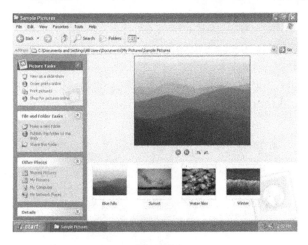

Fig.3.3

▶ Next place your mouse pointer on the picture, then *right click* on it. Remember when I say *right click* you have to place your finger on the right side of the mouse then click it one time. Does your screen look like the one below? Figure 3.4

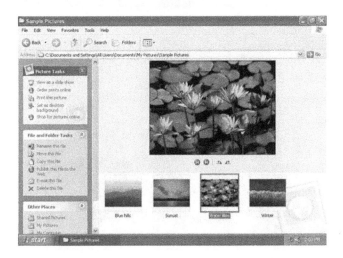

Fig.3.4

▶ Next place your mouse pointer on "set as Desktop Background". Then click it once, it will appear like the one below. Figure 3.5

▶ Second way, if you have a digital camera you can attach it on your computer through USB device. Like in the picture below. Figure 3.6

▶ Then follow the instruction on the screen to finish loading the pictures to your computer.

▶ The last step is Pictures CD. Just open the CD-Rom, insert your CD, and then follow up with the on screen instructions.

Fig.3.5

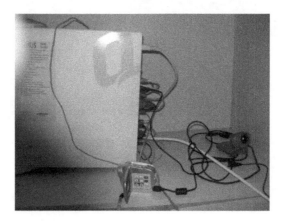

Fig.3.6

▶ The second way you can access the Display Properties is to click *start* that is on the left corner of your screen, then place the mouse pointer on the word settings. Then gently move it across to the words "Control Panel", click once. Then the drop box will appear like the one below. Figure 3.7

▶ Then left click on the words "Appearance and Themes" once. Does your screen look like the one below? Figure 3.8

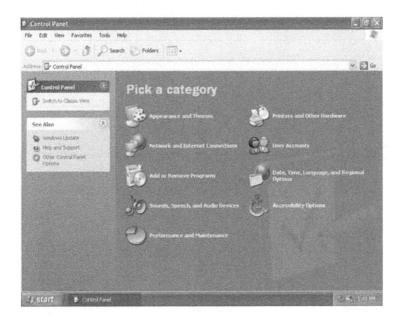

Fig. 3.7 & 3.8

▶ Next, click on Settings. You will be able to adjust the screen resolution. Does your screen look like the one below? Figure 3.9

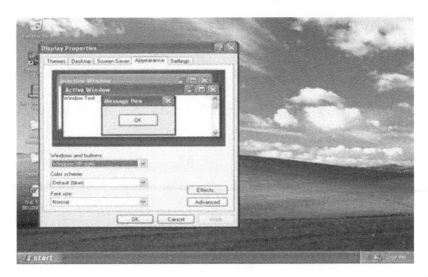

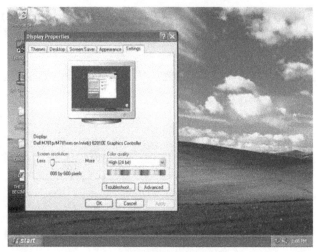

Fig.3.9

▶ If you are not satisfied with your on screen resolution the choice is yours. You can modify it as well.

▶ What is on screen resolution?

Answer—It is the size of the icons that appear on your computer's screen, small, medium or larger which is measure in pixel

▶ The More pixels, the smaller the icons. The less pixels the larger are your icons. Example: 800x600 pixels try it to see. Figure 3.9 from the previous page.

▶ Next try 1024x708 pixels. How do you enjoy it so far? It is fun? Take a stretch before you continue.

Computer is real fun. You are now in the land of adventure. Don't you? Certainly you are.

▶ Now let's draw a picture screen. Go to start that is on the bottom left corner of your screen, click once.

▶ Next position the mouse pointer on programs, then accessories, move the pointer gently across to the word "paint" that is on the third drop box as in figure 4.0

▶ Left click on the word paint then another drop box will appear like the one below, figure 4.1

▶ Now ready to make your artwork just move the mouse pointer on the screen it will appear like a crayon. Then press and hold the left side of the mouse as you make your drawing.

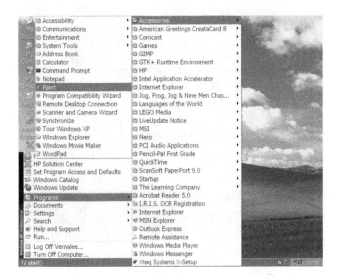

Fig.4.0

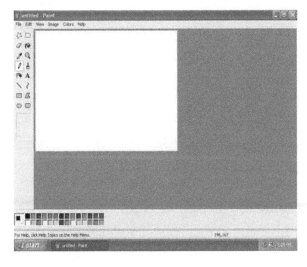

Fig.4.1

▶ After you have made your choice from the background list, make sure that under the word Position comes a little box. In it, you will see either the word Center, Tile or Stretch. You can click on the *blue box* under the word Position, choose the word Stretch then click Ok it will fill up the screen. See the figure below. 4.2

Fig.4.2

SET UP A SCREEN SAVER

You can set up your computer to display a screen saver when your PC is on but sits idle for a specified time. To do this, first select the Screen Saver tab in the Display Properties window.

▶ First use your middle finger to click on the right side of the mouse once, then in the drop box that appears gently move your mouse pointer to properties, use your index finger to click the left side of the mouse. Remember you have done it before.

▶ Now click screen saver that is the third words from the Display Properties

| Themes | Screen Saver | Desktop |

select a screen saver from the list by clicking on the blue box where windows XP is. See figure below. 4.3

▶ You will see your choice on the small screen in the window above it. To see how it looks on the full screen, click Preview. To return to the Display Properties window, just move your mouse.

▶ Next you can modify the speed or look of your screen saver by clicking on settings. Once you are happy with your choice, click Ok to return to the Display Properties Window. See figure 4.4

▶ Note that, windows offer many different screen savers: Flying through Space allows you to set different options including speed and the number of stars.

▶ Adjust the time before activating the screen saver, the numbers of minutes in the Wait box. The shortest time available is one minute. Click *Apply*, and then *Ok* to finish.

► You can also download a particular Screen Saver and save it on the desktop. Then install it on your system. Later in another chapter you will learn how to navigate on the Internet.

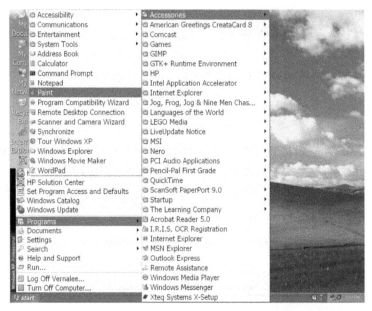

Fig.4.3

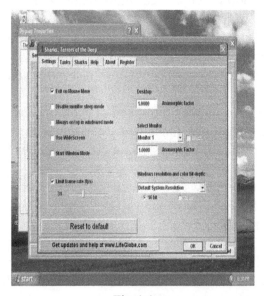

Fig.4.4

A book is a mirror: when a monkey looks in,
No apostle can look out.
By Geng Christoph

CHAPTER 2

Fig.5.0

KEYBOARD SHORTCUTS

Pointing and clicking the mouse is a friendly and easy way to control your PC. But if you are already typing, it is usually quicker to use the keyboard for certain commands. If you're typing a letter and want to save your work, reaching for the mouse, going to the file menu, and selecting save from the drop-down menu takes far more time and effort than pressing the control and S keys. Using the keyboard also maintains the rhythm of your typing.

Keyboard commands are easy to master. With a little practice they will soon become second nature and make you a fluent windows user. See figure 5.0 above.

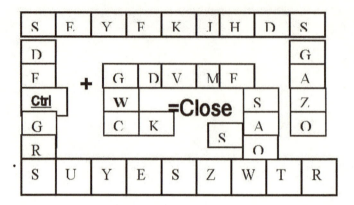

KEYBOARD

A Keyboard's primary function is to act as an input device. Using a keyboard, a person can type a document, use keystroke shortcuts, access a menu, play games and perform a variety of other tasks. Keyboards can have different keys depending on the manufacturer or the operating system it was designed for.

Most keyboards have between 80 and 110 keys including:

- ↑ Typing keys
- ↑ A numeric keypad
- ↑ Function keys
- ↑ Control keys

Typing Keys: These are keys with the letters of the alphabet that you use to type to form your words. (See keyboard above)

Numeric keypad: These keys are to the right of the keyboard with the numerals 0 through 9 on the pad. If the num lock key and its light is on the numeric pad is active. If the num lock light is off the symbols underneath the numerals are active.

Control Keys: a control key is a modifier key which, when pressed in conjunction with another key, will perform a special operation (for example, Control +Alt + Delete); similar to the Shift key, the Control key rarely performs any function when pressed by itself. The control key is located on or near the bottom left side of most keyboards. It is usually labeled *Ctrl*, but sometimes *Control* or *Ctrl* is seen.

Function keys: A function key is a key on a computer or terminal keyboard which can be programmed so as to cause an operating system command interpreter or application program to perform certain actions. On some keyboards/computers, function keys may have default actions, accessible on power-on. The function buttons are F1 to F12 located at the top of the keyboard.

Cursor Keys: These are the arrow keys found on your right of the keyboard. They move the cursor up and down, left or right on your screen.

Also in that section of the keyboard you will find the Insert, Home, Page Up, Delete, End and Page Down. The Page up and Page Down buttons allows you to move the page you are working on up or down or move the screen up or down. The Home button allows for the cursor to be placed at the beginning of the line you are writing in. The End buttons allows for the cursor to be placed at the end of the line you are writing in.

Enter: The Enter key is used to to begin another paragraph of your writing. So if you are typing your document the enter key will only be pressed if you reach the end of a paragraph and would like to start another.

Escape: The escape button located at the top left hand corner of the keyboard is very useful in microsoft word documents. It is used to escape from making mistakes. Pressing something that you did not mean to press, you can escape injury to your document by pressing the *Esc* button on your keyboard.

Caps Lock: This button located on the left of the keyboard is used for typing the document using capital letters. If the lock is on the letters typed will be in capital letters. If the lock is off the letters typed will be in lower case. If you want only the first letter in the word to be in capital letter, it is best to hold down the shift key and the letter you want in capital letter.

Space Bar: The space bar is used to separate the words in a sentence. It must be pressed once after completing a word.

Tab Key: This key is used to make indents in your paragraph. This can be pressed once or twice depending on the nature of your paragraph.

Using Delete and Backspace Keys: Using the Delete keys is to delete characters in front of the cursor and using the Backspace is to undo characters behind the cursor. For example, You are typing a word *manufacturing* and while typing you typed *"mani"* the cursor will be at the *i* then you would use the backspace key to erase and then type the *u*. If you were typing and you misspelt the word using *manupation* you would put the cursor between the *u and the p* by using the arrow keys and then press the delete key to erase the letters *pation* and then you would be able to type the remaining letters *facturing.*

The keyboard keys have many functions and you should be familiar with the keys as they can help you to be efficient and creative in using your personal computer.

Using the Shortcut Keys on the keyboard

There are many functions that the keyboard keys can do without the use of the mouse. This is done using the control key. Different application programs, user interfaces, and operating systems use the various control key combinations for different purposes.

K e y combination	What it Does	Command line and program read line
Crtl + A	Select all	Beginning of line
Crtl + B	Bold	Backward one character
Crtl + C	Copy	Copy present document to add to another
Crtl + D	Font window for word processing	Forward delete or end of input
Crtl + E	Center alignment	Centers the document
Crtl + F	Find usually a small piece of text in a larger document	Forward one character
Crtl + G	Go To window	
Crtl + H	Replace window	This replaces a word that you use in the document
Crtl + I	Italic	It italicizes words in the documents
Crtl + K	Insert Hyperlink	This is a hyperlink to the web
Crtl + M	Decreases margin by ½ inch in Microsoft Word	This executes the command
Crtl + N	New Document	A new page to start a new document
Crtl + O	Open	Allows you to look and open a document saved

Crtl + P	Print	Print window allowing for features of printing
Crtl + S	Save	Saves the document you are working on
Crtl + U	Underline	It allows for typing and underlining at the same time which must be pressed again after using
Crtl + V	Paste	This allows you to paste the document you copied
Crtl + Y	Redo	If by accident you deleted something it allows for redoing what was previously there
Crtl + Z	Undo	It undo actions done that was not meant to do
Crtl + End	Bottom of the Page	It allows you to automatically go the bottom of the document
Crtl + Home	Top of the Page	It allows you to to automatically go to the top of the document
Crtl + Alt + Delete	Task Manager	It allows for you to reboot your computer

Using the short cut keys allows for free movement using only the Keyboard. Shutting down your PC, you can use the keyboard. If you should touch the window key on your PC you will see the start menu. Press the U and the turn off manager appears. Press the U again it will turn off your PC. Sometimes when we touch the mouse our hand is so shaky that sometimes we cannot see the cursor on the monitor and therefore cannot handle cursor very well. Don't give up there are other ways for you to handle your PC.

Some books are to be tasted,
Others to be swallowed, and
Some few to be chewed and
Digested. By Francis Bacon

CHAPTER 3

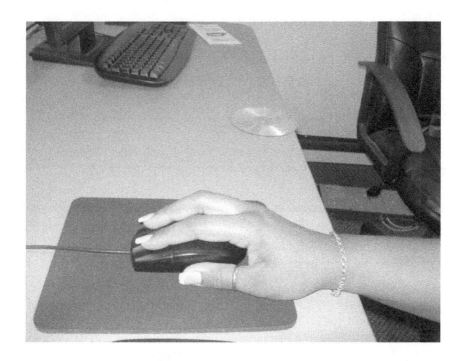

Fig. 5.1

USING YOUR MOUSE

First of all you should learn the rule of the mouse as a command input to the CPU. The CPU can be refered to as the brain. The monitor is refered to as the eyes. By looking at the eyes you are able to see what is happening and the information you would like the brain to store for you for later retrieval.

The mouse has two buttons located on the front of the mouse. One button is on the left and the other is on the right. The right hand is used to operate the mouse and the index finger is placed the left button and the middle finger of the right hand is placed on the right button. The rest of the fingers form a brace for the mouse. This gives you full control in using the mouse. Figure 5.1 give you an idea of how to handle the mouse.

When you are working with the mouse in a document the mouse pointer changes from a pointer to a cursor for typing purposes like this 'I' and it remains flashing on the screen. This allows for you to type your characters a letter at a time.

When you move the mouse on the task bar it changes from a cursor to a pointer indicating what it is you want to do. If you need to start a new document on a new page. You would move the mouse to the word File on the task bar and then you use the left mouse button to click for the drop down box to open. When the drop down box appears you move the pointer to New and then left mouse click and a new page will appear in front of you on your monitor with a flashing cursor ready for the input.

It is recommended that as you type your document you should try to save your work.

↑ To save your work you will move the mouse which appears as a pointer to the task bar and click on the word File and the drop down box will appear and then click on the word save.

↑ If it is the first time you are saving a document that you are working on the drop box will ask you to give the document a name. When you give it a name it is able to store it so that you can retrieve the document for later use.

↑ After you save the document and it has a name you can click on the little diskette at the top of the task bar to continue saving the document in that name. The diskette looks like this. Figure 5.2

Fig.5.2

If you would like to save the save document as a different name, you can click the save as in the File in the task bar menu. It is recommended that when you save a document you save it so that you can remember what is in the document.

> ➤ For example, you are typing up your resume, it would be recommended that you save the document as resume. Should you want more copies to be sent out you would open the document resume for easy retrieval.
> ➤ The CPU normally takes the first word or line that you typed in the document as a suggestion in saving. You donot have to take that suggestion, feel free to make your own or to accept.

Sometimes while typing your document you would like to see how it appears. Here are the steps you could do to view this:

> ✦ Click *File* from the task bar and look for Print Preview and left click on the mouse and the document will appear the way it will look when printed.
> ✦ This view allows you to preview before printing so that you will not waste paper and ink printing document. It gives you a chance to look at the document to make sure that is how you want it.
> ✦ To use the shortcut on the task bar look for the paper with the magnifying glass and then you use the left mouse click.
> ✦ If you so desire and you like the document you can go ahead and print the document.

HERE ARE THREE (3) DIFFERENT TYPES OF MICE YOU WILL ENCOUNTER:

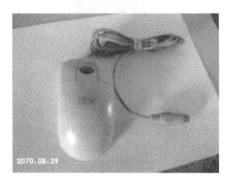

PS/2 MOUSE

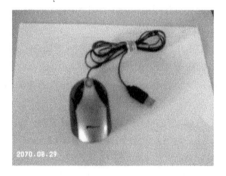

USB MOUSE

USB WIRELESS MOUSE

Most people, especially young, are comfortable with the function of a mouse. It anables you to select graphical items on a graphical screen. For many years, a dedicated mouse port did not even exist. Mice simply connected via either 9-pin or 25—pin serial ports. The acceptance of a mouse as an integral part of the PC, however, create a demand for the mouse to have its own connector, just as the keyboard had its own connector. In the mid—1980s, a new type of mouse connector made its debut with the introduction of the IBM PS/2 personal computer. Although still a serial port, the new PS/2—style dedicated mouse port used mini-DIN connector (see figure 5.3)

Keyboard Connector

Mouse Connector

Fig. 5.3

MOUSE TROUBLE SHOOTING

Keep your mouse or mice away from all dirty things. You can clean the mouse pad, wipe it with a clean soapy damp cloth, and use a peice of clean napkin paper to dry it, then place the mouse back unto it.

Your mouse should not give you problem. It can serve you for many years. However, because it has moving parts that may wear out. It may need to be replaced someday. But if it's happen, make sure that you know your mouse type or take the old one with you.

A malfunctioning mouse can be very frustrating. It can even bring your pressure at a higher level. You may think the computer itself is not good. Before you get panic, consider that you are facing a simple and easy-to-solve problem, for example a poorly maintained or dirty mouse or the cord may be slack from the back of the computer.

Such problem can be easily fixed with a few basic checks and adjustments.

MAKE SURE THE MOUSE CONNECTOR IS NOT SLACK

Once the mouse pointer does not move when you attempt to move it, the most likely cause is a loose of connection. Don't panic, there is nothing to shock you at the back of the computer. It is well protected against electrical shock.

► First turn off your computer. Then follow the wire from the mouse to the back of the PC. Gently pull it out, then reinsert it, make sure that it is well inserted. It is common for connections to get loose over time. See figure 5.4

▶ If your mouse pointer is sticking, jumping around the screen or behaving in an erratic way, it is likely that the mouse rollers are dirty. Follow this simple routine to keep your mouse clean and trouble-free.

1) Turn the mouse upside down and wipe away any visible dirt from the sides. See figure 5.5a & 5.5b
2) Twist the mouse ball cover on the bottom of the mouse. Pull it up away, and allow the ball that is inside of it to drop in your hand, it will not hurt you.
3) Use a clean tooth brush that is not in use, brush all dirt and other particles that may stick by the rollers. Do not use any sharp objects or commercial cleaning products.
4) Return the mouse ball to its socket and fit the mouse ball cover into position.

Tips—95% of the PC users rely on the mouse because, without it, they would have to use the keyboard for every command. Absolutely there is no problem with the mouse that cannot be traced to one of the two factors—a loose connection or a dirty mouse. So give your mouse and the pad a treat, quick cleaning on a regular basis. And never forget to check for loose cables behind your PC. Do not take the mouse by the cord because this puts stress on the cables. Gentle touch is the secret.

Fig.5.5a

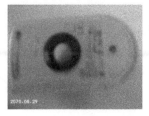

Fig.5.5b

PRINTING A DOCUMENT

Here you can use the shortcut key on the task bar or you can use the Print in the File task bar. Here is how you do it on the task bar menu.

↑ You click on the File on the task bar menu and in the drop down box use the pointer to click on the print. The only difference here is that a drop box appears after you click on the Print from the File task bar. It gives the option of choosing which printer that is, if you have more than one printer.

↑ After verifying the printer and if in case you need more than one copy of the document then you can select the number of copies by using the up and down arrow key beside the copies in the Print Box

↑ You also have the chance to print certain pages. Supposing you did a document containing five pages.

➢ You only select All if you want all of the five pages printed

➢ You only select Current if you only want the current page you are looking at in the document to be printed

➢ You only select Pages if you want selected pages to be printed. For example, you want pages 1, 3 and 5 to be printed. You would type 1, 3, 5 in the Pages section.

➢ After you have completed the steps above, move the mouse pointer to the OK button at the bottom of the Print menu and left mouse click and your document will be printed.

Printing from taskbar: This is done by using the mouse to click the picture of the printer from the task bar. The only difference with this is that the drop down box will not appear but it will automatically print all the pages in the document. You do not have the option to choose the page that you want unless you Print from the File menu. See figure 5.6

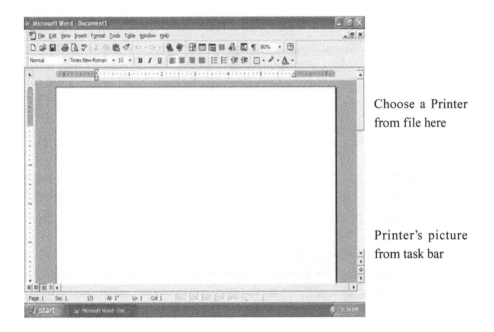

Choose a Printer
from file here

Printer's picture
from task bar

Fig.5.6

DEVELOPING YOUR DOCUMENT

The more advance you get in writing your document; you can develop your document by formatting it, by changing the way your letters in the document looks. What do I mean by changing the way your letters look in the document? Simply, you want the letters small, medium or large, or do you want your letters to look cursive or in script with curves or without curves. Changing the styles and size of the letters is called FONTS and FONT SIZE respectively. Here is how we change the Font and Font size.

- ♠ First, we move the mouse to the task bar to Format and left mouse click and a drop down menu box will appear. It is the first one in the line up Font. Click on Font and another drop down box will appear.
- ♠ In the Font box, you can choose which font you would want by scrolling the up and down arrow on the right and left mouse click.

  ➢ If you are writing a letter to a business place the suggested type face would be Times New Roman or Arial. You can choose as you go along and experiment to see which you want.

- ♠ In the Font style box there is an option to decide whether you want regular, bold, italics, or bold with italics. Click the style you want.
- ♠ In the size box you can choose the size of the letters. The sizes vary from smallest to largest, that is size 8 to 72. The smaller the number the smaller the letter size. The bigger the number the bigger the letter size.

  ➢ The recommended typed letter size is 12 or 14.

- ♠ The Font can be coloured. To suit the colour of the letters typed you can click on word or words that you want to be in coloured then drag the mouse across the word or words until it is black and release your hand off the mouse.

➤ Use the mouse to move to the task bar to Format then click on the word Font and the drop down menu will appear.

➤ Look for Font color and then select the arrow key and a color bar will appear. Select the color you would like then click OK at the extreme bottom of the Font drop down menu box. The word or words would be in the selected color.

➤ If you wish to return to the normal color, black, then select Format from the task bar and click on Font and select the arrow key and the color bar will appear. Select the color black or automatic and it will return to the selected colour.

🠕 If you wish to underline the heading in your document in a variety of ways these are the options that are provided. Here is what you do.

➤ Select the word or words to be underlined by clicking and dragging the mouse across the word or words you wish to be underlined until it is black which is called highlighting

➤ Move the mouse to the Format on the task bar and click.

➤ Select the Font in the line up and click.

➤ The drop menu will appear. Look for underline style. Choose whether you want to underline the word with a single line, a double line or wavy lines or dotted lines. Select the one that is applicable to you by clicking on the style you wish. Then click the OK button at the extreme bottom of the Font box. See figure 5.7, 5.7b, 5.7c

There are some special Effects that will help your document to look appealing. These effects can be found in the same Font box. How do we find it?

➤ Move the mouse to the task bar and click the Format on the task bar and then the Font is the first in the line up.

➤ In the Font drop down menu you will see the Effects and then you will click the box beside the one you want. Before you can use any of these the word or words that you want to take effect must be highlighted.

Here is a list of examples that would make the words in this sentence take effect. The sentence is: 'The brown fox is jumping.'

♠ *Example 1:* 'The brown fox is jumping.'-

➢ To turn the whole sentences into capital letters click the first letter at the beginning of the sentence and drag and hold the mouse to the end of the sentence.

➢ Then click the Format on the task bar. The drop down menu box will appear and then click on Font. See figure 5.8 and 5.9

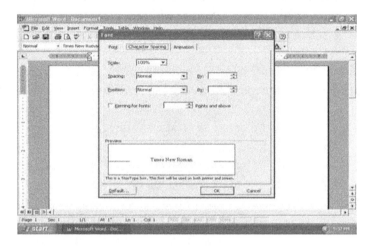

Fig.5.7

Fig.5.7b

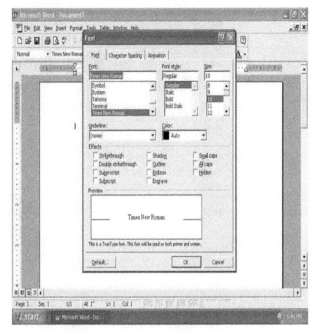

Fig.5.7c

Fig.5.8

First click format.
Then, the drop box for all
the features will appear.

This is the next drop
box you will see.

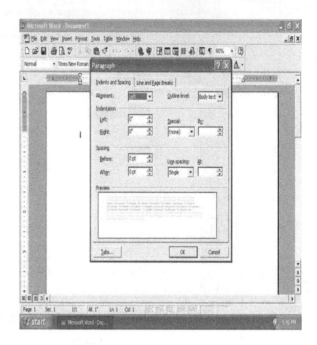

Fig.5.9

Then look for the EFFECT box and then ALL CAPS and tick the box
by left mouse click, then OK. All the letters will be in capital letters like
this: 'THE BROWN FOX IS JUMPING.'

> Then return to Font box and remove the tick from the box
> and click OK.
> *If you do not remove the tick every letter you type will take
> the same effect. Always remember to remove the tick after
> receiving the effect.*

♠ To have the sentence in small capital letters ALL (SM CAPS)
   follow the same steps in example 1 but tick the small caps box.
   It should look like this 'THE BROWN FOX IS JUMPING.'
♠ To have the sentence engraved follow the same steps in example
   one, but click on the Engrave box. It should look like this: '**The
   brown fox is jumping.**'

⬆ To have the sentence embossed followed the same steps in example 1 but tick the Emboss box. It should look like this: '**The brown fox is jumping.**'

⬆ To draw a line through a word it is done in the same way as you are doing. 'The brown fox is jumping.'-'The ~~brown~~ fox is jumping.'-

⬆ To draw a double line through a word it is done the same way as a above. 'The brown fox is ~~jumping~~.'-

⬆ The superscript is used for sending letters or numerals in the powers status. Example 2: If you were writing the name 'McKenzie'—You would highlight the 'c' alone and then click Format and then click the superscript. It should look like this: 'McKenzie' or 2^3 two to the third power.

⬆ The subscript does the opposite of the superscript and it is found in the same way as in Example 1. Let us look at 23 when subscript is turned on 2_3.

⬆ *Remember to turn off the effect after getting the effect otherwise all letters typed will be in the format selected*

ALIGNING YOUR DOCUMENT

There are four ways of aligning your document on the page. These are aligning the document by flushing the text to the left, centering your text in the document, aligning the document by flushing the text to the right or justifying the text in document on the page.

The symbols on the task bars are for easy retrieval of aligning your document.

> ➢ If you click on the icon on the task bar that looks like figure 6.0. It flushes the text to the left.
> ➢ If you click on the icon on the task bar that looks like figure 6.0. It will center the texts in the document.
> ➢ If you click on the icon on the task bar that looks like figure 6.0. It flushes the text on the document to the right.
> ➢ If you click on the icon on task bar that looks like this. It justifies the text on both sides of the page. See figure 6.0

Fig.6.0

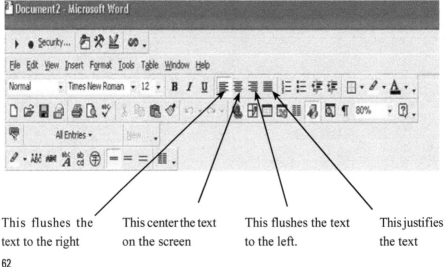

This flushes the text to the right   This center the text on the screen   This flushes the text to the left.   This justifies the text

LINE SPACING

When typing your document, you should pay special attention to the spacing between the lines. The spacing between line 1 and line 2 can be set. The Indent in your paragraph can be set along with run on sentences or with hyphenation or with hanging. Here is how you find the formatting of your paragraph.

- ↑ Move the mouse to Format task bar and click, and then click on paragraph. Here you will see the drop down menu bar.
- ↑ In this section you can adjust the spacing or the indenting of your paragraph.
- ↑ Once you set this, it becomes automatic when you click OK. Otherwise if you choose to change then go there and choose from this point forward. See figure 5.9 from the previous page.

USING THE TOOLS

It is useful that the computer is able to understand the English language better than you. Therefore it offers suggestions to you and tells you when you type it is fragments or try to revise or say what you are typing another way. It also gives you suggestion in spelling words that you do not know how to or remember how to spell. This computer also gives similar words or synonyms for words from the thesaurus. All this and more can be accessed from the Tools on the task bar. Here is what you do.

> Click on the Tools on the task bar and then click Spelling or you may choose to press F7 on the keyboard as a shortcut which allows for the spelling to be checked.
> The spelling drop down box appears and the misspelled or unknown word (s) appears highlighted in your text on the screen. The box displays the misspelled word and suggests alternative spellings for most of them correct. Figure 6.1

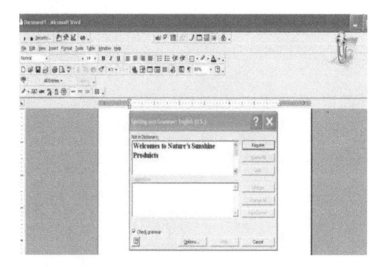

Fig.6.1

=

> ➤ If the highlighted word is correct, you can click the ignore button to skip over the word without making any changes.
> ➤ If you want to add a word to the spell check dictionary then you can click add?
> ➤ If you have more than one word spelt incorrectly in the document you can click on change all and it will change all the words. For example, if you misspell a word 'colour' with the 'u' spell check can change all the color you spelt with the 'u' to without the 'u' by clicking on the change all.
> ➤ When spell check has completed checking every word in every line and it is done a box will appear saying 'spell check is completed'. Then click Ok.

USING TABLES

The table is used to line facts in rows and columns.

To carefully create a table in your document, simply follow these steps.

- ♠ Move the mouse to the table task bar and click and then a drop down menu bar will appear.
- ♠ If you know how many columns you want and how many rows you require for your table then click on the Insert and then on Table and fill in the number by using the scroll bar on the left then click OK to get the table inserted in your document.
- ♠ If you need more rows then you would put the cursor where you would want the row to be and then click on Table then click on Insert and then click on whether row or column needed; in this case it would be a row to be inserted then click OK. For example below are four rows and four columns. Figure 6.2 and 6.2a

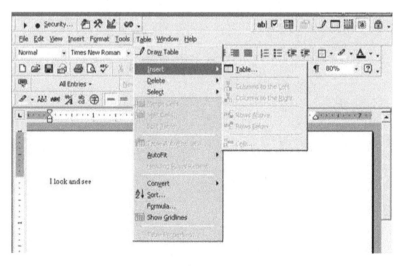

Fig. 6.2

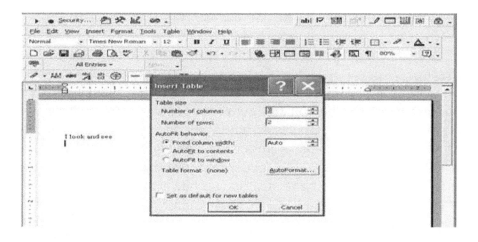

Fig.6.2a

Column 1	Column 2	Column 3	Column 4

Row 1			
Row 2			
Row 3			
Row 4			

USING COLUMNS

To start column(s) in your documents here is what you should do.

➢ Move the cursor on the document page where you want the column to start.

➢ Choose the Format on the task bar and click Columns and then you can choose whether you want one or more columns in your document. If you need more than what is designed there then click on the numbers of column box. Two columns are better advised to work with, as you are readily able to read the two columns. More columns you use would make the text skinner and less attractive and may be harder to read.

➢ If you want to start a new column from where you are now, click the new start column box. This will allow for a column break in the document.

➢ Click the Apply To drop down menu and click the apply the columns to the whole document or just from now on, which is from this point forward. Then click Ok.

Fig.6.3

ADDING PICTURES

Sometimes when creating your document you would like to add pictures from the computer. These pictures are called clip art and can be inserted in the document.

➢ First we click on the Insert on the task bar and then click on picture. Then another dropping will appear, you will see, ClipArt, from file and so on. If you have some personal pictures save on the system, you may want to click from file to access it, if not the only alternative is to click on ClipArt. See figure 6.4 and also see figure 6.5 below.

➢ Once you are there the pictures are placed under different category.

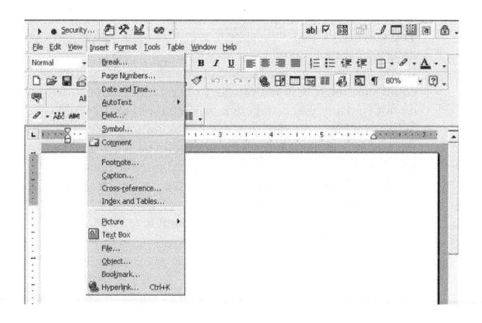

Fig. 6.4

Fig.6.5

Determine what it is you want and then all the pictures in that category will appear.

> The categories that will appear are: communication, cartoon, nature, home and so on.
> If you are looking for a picture of someone shaking hands you could start looking in the category of communication and if you do not find any you could click on keep looking.
> When you have found what you are looking for you can click on the picture and then click on the insert clip on the drop down box beside the picture and it will be inserted into the document.
> Then you right mouse click on the picture and the format picture drop down box will appear.
> Click on layout tab and view the different layouts

ORGANIZING YOUR PICTURE

After you view the layout of the picture you can select the one which best describes how you want the layout. Let us look what happens if we select each of the layout to format the picture we have selected.

❖ If you have selected the in line with text layout, this will be the format.

What will happen is the picture will hide some of the words printed. In this one you will have to put the picture first and then write what you want underneath it or beside the picture.

This is a good picture of good communication at the work place.

We can see that this will develop in a healthy relationship or agreement to work together. In order to get the picture to increase or reduce in size, click on the picture until little boxes around the box is highlighted that you can stretch the picture by putting the cursor in the corner of the small box (bottom right) and until the cursor turns diagonal then click and pull to increase. To reduce, you will have to click and pull inward.

❖ If you would like the picture to be placed in the middle of the document without shifting your document out of place, click on the square picture that shows how it will look in the document.

This is a picture of good communication at the work place. We can see that this will develop in a healthy relationship or agreement to work together.

USING WORD ART

❖ Word Art is a creative way of designing your document. You could create flyers or advertisement using word art.

❖ To find Word Art, you must click on the Insert in the task bar and then position the mouse pointer on the word Picture and then gently move the mouse pointer across, then down to the word Art then click on it once, then the drop down menu will appear. See figure 6.6

Fig.6.6

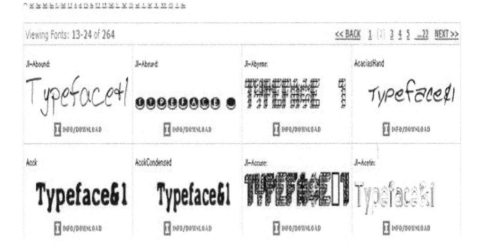

Fig.6.6a

- ❖ You will have a variety of styles to choose from. You must first look at the style to see which one will fit the design you so desire.
- ❖ When you see the one you like the best click on that design then a text box will appear, then you can start to write your own text to fit that style.
- ❖ When you are finished writing your text click the OK box at the bottom and then you will have your style designed.

For example: The word communication can be written in different styles.

Color can be changed when you click on the word
And Word Art edit box appears just in case if you
Wanted to change your text. Both for the
Outline and the fill in color.

Fig. 6.7

There is no need to worry about your drawing. Microsoft Paint is the Technology you need. Use it any time you need it. How to access it? Click start, put the mouse pointer on All Programs, then Accessories, and then gently move the mouse pointer across and down to the word Paint, click it once. There you are.

Paint provides different brush sizes and styles and it offers many different colors and shapes for you to choose from. Also Paint makes it simple to correct you composition or change anything in your drawing.

It is amazing and fun, be patient in doing your work and practice make perfect.

Tips—Just before you use Paint, take a self-guided tour around the icons in the toolbar to find out what they do. Move the cursor over each tool and a label will pop up to tell you the name of the tool. If you look at the bottom of your screen, you will see a brief description of that tool.

FINDING PICTURES

The adventurous can draw their own pictures, using a paint program. But you can also buy CDs that include Clip Art images like American Greetings CreataCard. Figure 6.8. If you have access to the Internet, you can use a search engine to look for web sites that offer free clip Art that you can download. Make a clip art folder on your hard drive to store them in.

After you have created one or more cards, you can start to design a unique one for your special purpose. Use the ClipArt and WordArt features found in Works and Word pictures. Find or take photos of family and relative, then scan them into your computer, if you don't have a digital camera, you can also scan it through your scanner or just place the picture on the front of the greeting card template and add a special message to reflect the occasion. A picture means lots to friends and relatives whom you haven't seen for a while. See figure 6.9

Fig.6.8

Fig.6.9

Books are the quietest and most
Constant of friends; they are the
Most accessible and wisest of counselors,
And the most patient of teachers.
By Charles W.

CHAPTER 4

START A PROGRAM

In windows, you can use the keyboard instead of the mouse to provide instructions to your computer. You can even open the start menu and launch programs using keys only. Now, let us navigate using the keyboard:

Start

1-. To open the Start menu, press the windows key, next to the Control (Ctrl) key on your keyboard. Then press the Up arrow key on the right of your keyboard. Notice how this highlights options farther up the menu. Keep pressing the Up arrow until you have highlighted Programs at the top of the menu then press "enter" to execute the command.

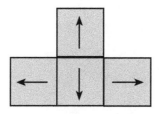

Fig.7.0

Press the "Down arrow" To scroll down through
The menus. Press the "Up arrow," to scroll up.

2-. If you don't see a windows key on your keyboard. You still can access the start menu. Just press Ctrl+Esc (the Esc key is in the top left corner of your keyboard). The arrow will work the same way.

trlC + Esc

3-. Gently press the Right arrow key once to reveal the submenu for the Programs menu. Arrow keys allow you to move up and down the submenus, also. To move back to the start menu, press the left arrow key. Try navigating to Microsoft FrontPage. Press enter.

4-. For example if it's happen to be running several programs at once, you can move between them using (Alt + Tab) Hold down the Alt key and press Tab. You can then Tab from Program to Program, selecting the one you want.

LEARNING NEW SHORTCUTS

It's easy to pick up new shortcuts to help you work more quickly. You have a ready reference aid on screen. Use the mouse to click on the tools menu. You'll notice that some choices in the drop-down menu have keyboard equivalents.

In both Microsoft works and Word, F7 is to call the spellchecker.

WORKING WITH DOCUMENTS

There are many shortcuts similarities to most windows programs; it's good to learn them. Some of the most common shortcuts are shown here. They are easy to remember because the key you press after the Control key is often the first letter of the action you want. For example, (Ctrl + P) to print (Ctrl + S) to save a document.

1-. To open a new document in Microsoft Word
Press Ctrl + N.

1-. My sister opens menus using the keyboard shortcut. How is this done? To view one of the top menus in most programs, press Alt plus the underlined letter in the menu you want. For example, Alt + 1 open the insert menu. When options in a drop-down menu include underlined letters, type this letter select them, for example, *B* to select Page Break in the Insert menu.

2-. Can l open folders using shortcuts?
Yes, in windows you can use the arrow keys to move from folder to folder (or file), in an open window. Type the first letter of any folder to highlight it. To select another folder to the right, press the Right arrow key; to select a folder below, press the down arrow,

and so on. Open a highlighted folder by pressing the enter key. It is possible to move around the desktop in a similar way, opening my Computer by highlighting it and pressing, "Enter."

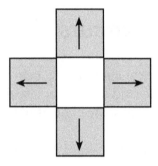

3-. My friend told me there is a quick way to undo mistakes using only the keyboard?
Yes, you can always type Ctrl + Z to undo your last action. To "undo an undo" in Works, press Ctrl + Z a second time. This key command is used in many windows programs.

HOW TO CONVERT PICTURES FROM MICROSOFT WORDS OR WORKS TO JPEG WITH A RESOLUTION OF NO LESS THAN 300 DPI?

This has been a problem for many people both in the business sector and in the homes. Some think that they should have special software to make the conversion; while others think it is a magical touch. The more you read, the more you'll learn, the more intelligent you'll become. In a few minutes this secret is going to be revealed to you. Not only are you going to know how to do the conversion, but also how to use your own keyboard to take pictures of your screen. No need for a digital camera, or camcorder, nothing to scan or insert, just the keyboard the screen and the mouse you need to use.

Now suppose I am working on Disk Management and I want to take a picture and print it. First let's elaborate a little on Disk Management console in windows 2000 and XP enables you to partition and format drives, and it also makes it work almost the same like Disk Administrator in windows NT 4.0. You can create multiple primary partitions and an extended partition with logical drives. See figure 7.1 for more detail.

First right click on My Computer, and then click on Manage, next click on Disk Management. Now I am going to take the picture to place it in the document. Take a look at your keyboard. Let's explore the very first row of keys. To your right hand side the first key is Pause/break, then comes Scroll lock, then *"Print Screen/SysRq"*. This is the key you need, make sure that the Computer Management is shown on the screen then press the "Print Screen/SysRq" see figure 7.2 below.

Fig.7.1

This is the key you
Need to press now. It mark:
Print Screen
SyrsRq

Fig.7.2

Next open Microsoft word or works whatever is installed in your computer, then click "Edit" and then "Paste". There you are; can you see it? You can play around or modify it as you wish. See figure 7.3 on the following page.

Now let us convert this picture to JPEG file with a resolution of 300 dpi or more. Go to file at the top left hand side, click "Print Preview." Next go to All Program, position the mouse pointer on "Accessories" then select "Paint" next on your keyboard press the Control (Ctrl) key together with the letter "V." Next to your left hand side at the top you will see a few shapes just the one next to the star is a square, position the mouse pointer on it and click it. You can use that feature to select whatever you want from the present picture you are working.

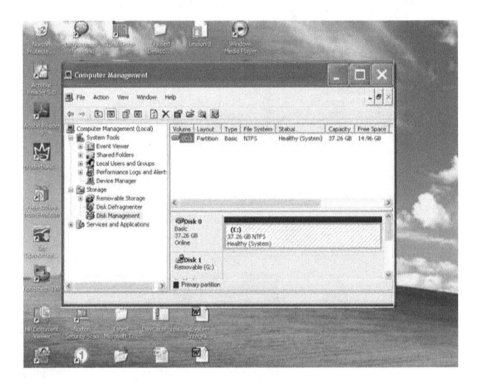

Fig.7.3

Now go to "File" that is on the screen at the top left corner click it, then select "Save as." Then you will see another dropping like the one in the figure 7.4 below.

Choose where you want it to be saved. Is it on your desktop or in your document, then "File name" give it a name, next "Save as type" click on the blue arrow to make your selection. There are different choices. Now click on JPEG then click save. You have done it.

Next step open the CD-Rom Drive insert a blank CD then right click on file name where you have saved the picture, then click copy and then open the My computer icon, right click on the CD-Rom drive where you place the blank CD then click "Paste".

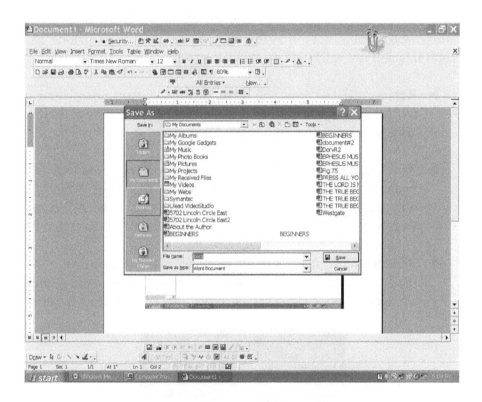

Fig.7.4

WHY IS IT THAT SOMETIMES MY CD-ROMS

DON'T WORK?

The CD-ROMs and drives are very reliable. This doesn't mean that things cannot go wrong sometimes. We do have cases where the drive itself fails, and other time is the CD itself. So you will need to check the CD itself carefully to see if there is any scratch on it or if it is dirty. Before calling a technician, first follow this procedure. After you have done your best if it is still not working you can call a technician to fix it for you.

► Remove the CD from the drive, analyze it carefully, if there is any scratch or trace of dirt, use a clean piece of white soft cloth, wipe it in a circular motion until it is clean.

► Now insert the CD in the drive if it still don't play you will need to buy something call "CD LASER LENS CLEANER" which you will find in any computer's store, Walgreen pharmacy, CVS, and Family dollar store as well. It looks like this one in the figure 7.5

► If the problem is really in the drive you will not be able to open it with the button on the CD-ROM DRIVE. There is a secret now it is going to unveil to you. Use the manual way to eject the CD from the drive.

Fig.7.5

DVD, CD Lens
cleaner

▶ Look carefully at the front of the drive, just an inch below it, to your right hand side. There it is, gently insert a straightened paper clip or a pin into the hole to release the tray and the CD-ROM will pop open right away. See figure 7.6

Fig.7.6

▶ just before you do this make sure that your PC is well grounded, and that you are correctly inserting the CD into the tray. They should be level in the recessed circle and the label must be facing up. See figure 7.7

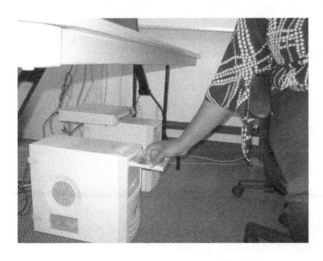

Proper way to insert your CD and DVD into the drive

Fig.7.7

RECOGNIZING A BAD DISC

If you cannot get your software to load form the CD-ROM, you may have a problem with the disc itself, rather than with your PC. Work through these steps to solve basic problems.

▶ If you get a "not ready" message when you try to view the contents of a CD, try loading another CD. If the same problem or error persists, check that your PC recognizes your specific CD drive.

▶ If you have access to another computer try the same CD on it just to make sure where the problem lies. Then if you receive the same message. The Disc is faulty. Return it where you purchase it.

▶ Now checking your CD-ROM drive type. Double click on My Computer icon, and then position your mouse pointer on the CD DRIVE (D) icon. Like in the figure 7.8 in the following page.

▶ Next use your middle finger to right click on the CD-ROM drive, another dropping will pop-up like figure 7.9 next page.

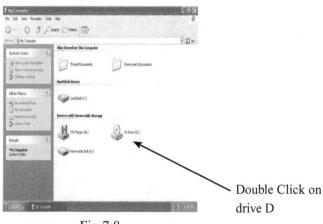

Double Click on drive D

Fig.7.8

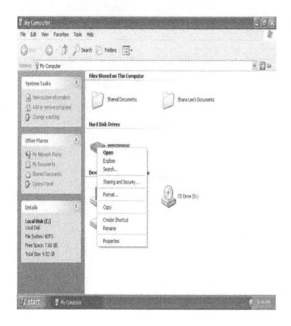

This is how it will appear.

Fig.7.9

▶ Next click on properties and then watch the screen. Does it look like the one below? Figure 8.0

Fig.8.0

▶ Next click AutoPlay beside General. Like in the figure below. Then make your correction if necessary.

▶ Now, click on Hardware. You will see the name for the CD-ROM drive. See figure 8.1 and 8.2

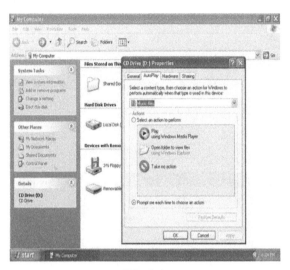

Fig.8.1

Fig.8.2

INCREASE DISK SPACE

This is another important feature to know about because every time you use your computer to store files, like letters, things you download from the Internet, database, and whatever, take up more disk space. The programs and games you install also occupy valuable space from the drive.

▶ Storing everything on your hard disk is like putting your books on the bookshelf. When it is full, that is it; you won't be able to add any more unless you make more space on the shelf. Sometimes to make space you will have to take off those you are not using at the moment. Don't you?

▶ So it is similar to the hard disk. Cleaning up your hard disk will give you room to add others. Do not discard files randomly. You might delete something that you or the other user or your friend may need at a later date.

▶ Keep an eye on how much disk space you have by double-clicking on My Computer icon and selecting Properties from the files menu. See figure 8.3 in the following page.

REMOVE PROGRAMS

Once you notice your disk space is about to be full. It makes sense to remove old files that is not in use for new once.

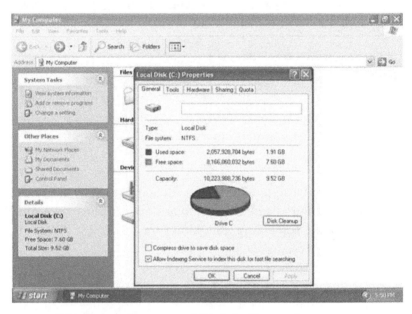

Blue is used space and Pink indicates free space.

Fig.8.3

▶ Now if you don't have Uninstall program, click on start, gently move your mouse pointer to Control Panel, then click add/ remove program icon.

▶ The Add/Remove Programs Properties window appears. Click on the program you would like to uninstall to highlight it, and then click on Remove, then follows the instruction to the end. It will run for about 2 minutes. When it is finished you will be asked to restart your computer. See figures 8.4

Fig.8.4

Next Clear Out Unwanted Files—Search for files that you have not used for a while and you no longer want them. Then get rid of them, especially files that contain pictures will free up lots of space because graphic files are usually large.

▶ From the start button, position your mouse pointer on all programs, then gently move it across to Accessories, drag it across again to window explorer, and click it once. See the figure below. Figure 8.5

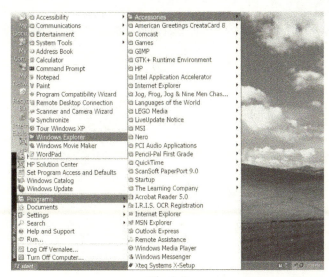

Fig.8.5

▶ Click on any folder in the left hand side of the window to view its contents, then, double-clicks folders on the right hand side to view inside of them.

▶ To sort your documents so that the oldest are on the top, go to the View menu and select Details. Then click the Modified tab beside the list of files. Resize the window to see more dates if necessary. See figures 8.6 and 8.7

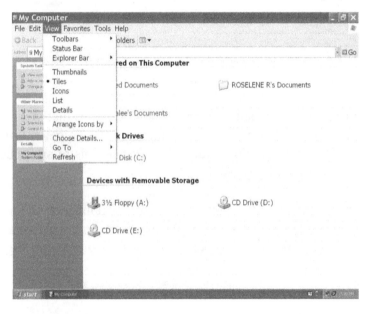

Fig.8.6

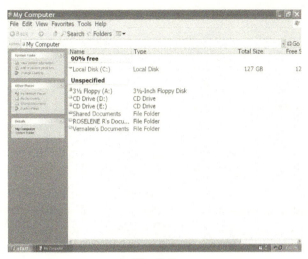

Fig.8.7

▶ Next step. Drag-unwanted files to recycle bin, then release your mouse button. To delete multiple documents, hold down the Ctrl key as you click on files. When you have made your selection, drag the files into Recycle bin and release the mouse button. See figure 8.8

Fig.8.8

Write and Print a Letter

Writing and printing letters with your computer is not only a good way to handle your correspondence; it's a good way to build up your PC skills, too. You'll quickly learn how to create and work with documents, save, and file them out with ease.

You'll also learn how to use the keyboard, how to style and lay out a letter, as well as shortcuts for the various word-processing program features. At the same time, you will become familiar with the mouse and printer functions.

Although this may sound like a lot at once, there's no need to worry. Take as much time as you need and remember that there's nothing wrong in making a mistake. It's often the best way to learn.

OPEN NOTE PAD OR MICROSOFT WORD

You can prepare a letter in note pad or Microsoft word. Open note pad or Microsoft word; position the mouse pointer on start that is at the bottom left of your PC click it once. Then positions the mouse pointer on all program do not click hold it in position, then the program will open.

▶ Look for Microsoft word or Microsoft office, if you see Microsoft office but not words then position your mouse pointer on Microsoft office, then Microsoft word will appear in another column. Click it once watch your screen. Does it look like the one below? See figures 8.9

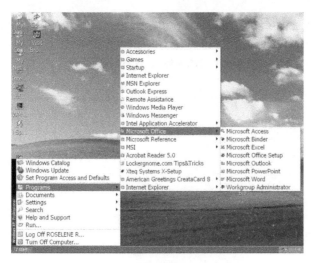

Fig.8.9

▶ Then the window will appear like in figure below, now ready to type your letter. Figure 9.0

▶ However if you don't have Microsoft office installs in your PC the only one you will have access to, is notepad, use the same procedure put your mouse pointer on all program look for accessories gently take your mouse pointer across to the word accessories, then click on Notepad. See figure 9.1

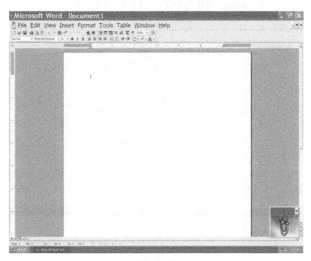

Fig.9.0

▶ then, another drop box will appear, gently move your mouse pointer across to the word notepad, and then click on it once. Ready to type your letter (see figure 9.1)

Fig.9.1

Microsoft word allow space on each page for headers and footers—that is, information that appears at the top and bottom of the page, Remember that any text in these sections will be printed on every page.

▶ Type your address and phone number, start each on a new line. Make sure you are not typing in the header section. See figure 9.2

Fig.9.2

▶ To get to the header and the footer, you click on View on the task bar and look for header and footer and then click. The header box will appear and you can type the information you want to see at the top of the page there. The information you want to see at the bottom of the page click the switch between header and footer and the footer will appear. Then type the information. Then click close when you are finished.

To position your address on the right, highlight it, and click the tool bar's right align button that is on the top of your screen the third box after the *U*.

ADD SOME STYLE

There are dozens of fonts available. Try out several to find which ones you like the best.

To choose a font, highlight your address, and telephone number using the mouse, then click on the down arrow next to the Times New Roman font on the tool bar. A list of fonts will appear. View them by scrolling up and down using the mouse pointer. Select by clicking on it. Click anywhere on the letter to confirm the change. See figure 9.3

Fig.9.3

Select a size for your address. Highlight it, and then click on the arrow next to the 12 on the tool bar. Click on the size you want. Do the same for your telephone number. You can make text bold or underlined by highlighting it, then clicking on the B or the u buttons in the tool bar. (See figure 9.4)

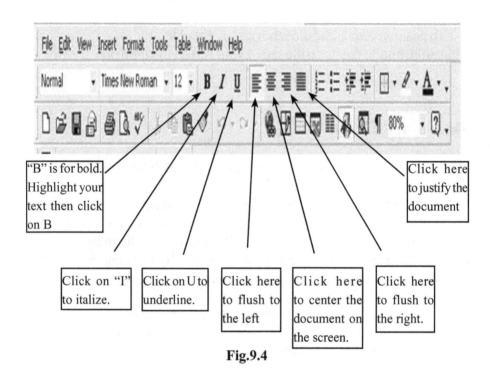

Fig.9.4

ADD A DATA TO YOUR TEXT

Now that you've got the look you like, it's time to write your letter. We'll start by inserting today's date in your letter, and then we'll begin to work with the body of the text.

At the top left hand side of your screen the fourth word to your right is "insert" click it once then click the words date and times once and it will be inserted. Now type the main text of your letter. If you accidentally type a couple of sentences or paragraph of text in the wrong place and want to move it, simply highlight it by dragging the cursor over the words you want to move. Then go to edit menu and select cut. Click where you want the text to go, then select Paste from Edit menu to reposition the text exactly where you want it.

Next step you don't want to loose you document now click save as. Go to file, which is the first words at the top left of your screen click once then look for "save as" click once.

Now you are ready to print your letter just before you do so check the overall look of the letter by selecting Print Preview from file menu. This shows you exactly how your letter will look when it is printed out. See figure 9.5

FINAL TOUCH

Now you can print your letter. Select print from the file menu. Check that the number of copies is one, so you are not wasting paper, and click ok. A box may appear, telling you the status of the printing process. When the job progress bar reaches 100%, your letter is printed. If you are using an Inkjet printer, allow the ink to dry before handling the printed letter. (See figure 9.6)

Fig.9.5

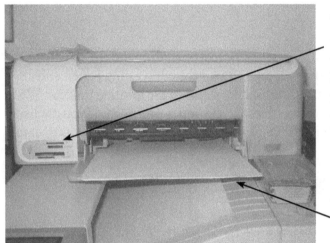

These are cards slots from your digital camera you can insert here and print your pictures without a computer.

Load paper here.

Fig.9.6

Natural abilities are plants,
That need pruning by study.
By Francis B.

CHAPTER 5

TEACH YOURSELF HOW TO TYPE

Amazing, I can't believe that I could do it myself. Of course you can. Every body has the potential to teach himself or herself somehow or another. The fact is "discipline."

In order to succeed in anything, you should discipline yourself. Choose the right Attitude. Key words: Believe that you can do it. Dream about it, and reach for it (or act upon it). Be consistent, and persistent. You are not a failure until you give up. Practice makes perfect.

Now you need to set some times to practice your typing skills. It doesn't have to be long, 30-45 minutes is enough? Do it on a regular basis.

Place your left little finger over the "A" key, your left ring finger over the "S" key, your middle finger over the "D" key and your left index finger over the "F" key. Now place your right index finger over the "J" key, your middle finger over the "K" key, your ring finger over the "L" key, and your little finger over the ":" key. And your thumbs will hit the space bar. Always return your fingers to the home row keys after reaching to type other letters. See figure 9.7

After you have trained your fingers. It is now the opportunity to add some speeds. Have your digital clock or a watch beside you. Set the number of minutes you want to try; but do not stress yourself, make fun. For example; the first time you set 10 minutes for 20 words and so on it's depend on you.

Fig.9.7

WHERE IS THE SPELLCHECKER ON MY PC AND HOW DO I USE IT?

There is a spellchecker in both Microsoft works and word. Use it when you've finished a letter or to check a particular word. To start the spellchecker, put the cursor at the beginning of your letter and choose spelling from the tools menu. The checker will move through your letter, suggesting corrections. It can also be accessed with the F7 key.

CAN I COPY TEXT FROM ONE LETTER TO ANOTHER?

Yes. To copy text from one document to another, open the document you want to copy and highlight the text you want, by holding down the left mouse button and dragging the mouse across it. Select Copy from the edit menu or hold down the Ctrl key and the letter C at the same time. In the new document, place the cursor where you want to insert the text. Select Paste from the Edit menu and your text will be copied.

I CAN'T GET MY LETTER TO FIT ON ONE PAGE. WHAT CAN I DO ABOUT THIS?

Sometimes lines spill onto a new page. Fit it all on one page by reducing the type size. Highlight the text; click the arrow next to the type size (usually 12) on the toolbar and click on a small size. Or delete some white space.

Page Setup: This has to do with the layout of your page. How do you want the page to look. Landscape is turning the paper width—wise and portrait is turning the paper length—wise or custom size. You would also want to check your margins around the paper and to make sure it is aligned properly.

This has to do with the layout of your page. How do you want the page to look. Landscape is turning the paper width—wise and portrait is turning the paper length—wise or custom size. You would also want to check your margins around the paper and to make sure it is aligned properly.

Print Preview. An onscreen view of what your page looks like when it is printed. This feature helps you judge whether the layout of your document is pleasing to the eye. This lets you make changes before printing and one way of saving paper!

Print Quality. The different ways your printer can print out the same letter or document, for example "draft" or "letter" quality. Choose the one most suited to your purpose, and remember that the lowest quality uses the least ink.

Resolution. The degree of fine detail with which your work is printed. Resolution is measured in dots per inch (dpi).

WORKING WITH WORDS

USING MICROSOFT WORD TOOLBAR

The toolbar in most word packages, including Microsoft Works, Office, and Word, is real time-saver-shortcuts allow you to do tasks that would otherwise take several steps using the drop-down menus.

HOW IT WORKS

The toolbar is the line of small boxes and buttons at the top of your word window—each one has its own icon. You can use these to change the size and style of your text, arrange text on the page, check your spelling, print and save your work, and more. Many of the buttons, such as Cut, Copy, and Paste, appear in other Windows programs, so once you learn how to use them for Microsoft word or works, you'll find them easy to use in other programs, too.

The Toolbar Explained

PERSONALIZE YOUR TOOLBAR

You can customize the toolbar's functions. By adding or removing buttons. Click on the Tools menu and select Customize Toolbar. There are several categories of Toolbar buttons. To add a button to the toolbar, click and drag it from the toolbar buttons box and drop it onto the toolbar. To remove a button, click it and drag it off the toolbar.

WHAT HAPPEN IT IS JUST SIX MONTH SINCE I BOUGHT THIS COMPUTER NOW IT IS NOT WORKING?

After a while the mouse may malfunction and it can be frustrating, I have seen it happen already, but be patient, don't loose your cool. The more frustrated you are, the more aggravating is the problem.

▶ This kind of problem can be easily fixed with a few basic checks and adjustments. You may even find that you can set up your mouse better than the way it came from the factory.

▶ Turn off your computer then Follow the wire from the mouse to the back of your computer. Even if the plug appears to be tightly connected, take it out and reinsert it.

▶ Often times the connection become loose. So make sure that the plug is pushed in safely and then any screw connections are finger—tight.

CHANGE THE FONT AND TYPE SIZE

These boxes allow you to change the style and size of your text.

1—Highlight the block of text you wish to change. Click on the down-arrow to the right of each box to reveal list of font and size options.

2—Scroll through the options; use your mouse and the scroll bar or by using the arrow keys on your keyboard.

3—Click on an option to highlight it, and the text will change to the font or type size you have chosen.

4—or place your cursors where you'll like your new text style to begin. Select your font and point size.

STYLE YOUR TEXT

These buttons allow you to format or style your text for a professional look. When you have finished typing, think about formatting your text so particular words or sections stand out for emphasis.

Highlight the text you want to change, then click on the appropriate toolbar button. If you haven't selected any text when you click the toolbar button, the change will take effect from the cursor's position on the page when you begin typing.

QUICK WAYS TO EDIT

The Cut, Copy, and Paste buttons allow you to edit your document easily by moving single words or entire sections of text. See figure 9.8

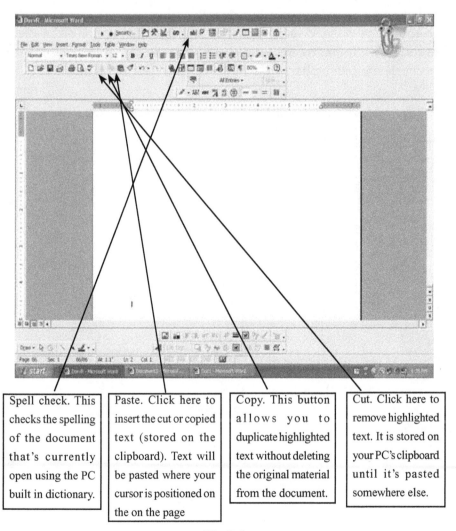

| Spell check. This checks the spelling of the document that's currently open using the PC built in dictionary. | Paste. Click here to insert the cut or copied text (stored on the clipboard). Text will be pasted where your cursor is positioned on the on the page | Copy. This button allows you to duplicate highlighted text without deleting the original material from the document. | Cut. Click here to remove highlighted text. It is stored on your PC's clipboard until it's pasted somewhere else. |

Fig.9.8

I want to make the font I am using 13 points, but that size isn't listed in the drop-down menu. How can I do it?

If you're using a True Type font (you can tell because it will have "TT" to the left of it in the drop-down menu), you can type the size you want into the point size box, type in your preferred size (between 4 and 127), then press Enter.

How can I use the toolbar to import pictures from Microsoft draw into my word document?

Go to the tools select customize toolbar. Select the list category then click on and drag the Microsoft draw button onto your toolbar.

Is it possible to temporarily hide my toolbar?

Yes. Go to the view menu and click on the toolbar option—the check beside it will disappear. To get the toolbar back, repeat the process and the check and the toolbar will reappear.

TROUBLESHOOTER

Fig.9.9

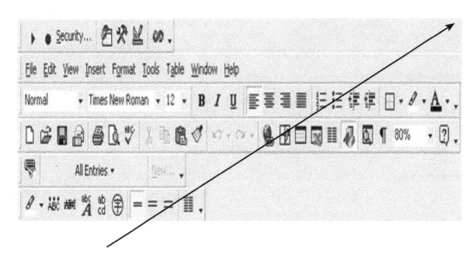

Part of your toolbar is missing. You may not be able to see the whole toolbar if your window does not fill your entire screen. "Maximize" the window by clicking on the middle button (the square) in the top right corner.

If you still can't see all of the toolbar, then you've got too many buttons on it. Remove some of the buttons you use least (see "Personalize your toolbar" on the front of this card) and access those commands from the drop-down menus.

Natural ability without Education has
More often attained to glory and Virtue
Than Education without natural ability.
By Cicero

CHAPTER 6

HOW TO INSTALL A NEW SOFTWARE ON YOUR COMPUTER?

Let's install your new printer I must tell you that there are two ways to install a printer. But I only elaborate on one way for now.

▶ The phrase setup the printer means to connect and configure it so that the system can relate to each other.

▶ Set—up procedures depend on whether the printer is connected to the local system, to a print server or straight to a network.

▶ The next activity is to troubleshoot and maintain a printer that is already installed. There are different types of printers though I am going to focus on one type alone but I will mention the different types that are in the market.

▶ The Dot Matrix Printers, Ink Jets Printers, and the Laser Printers.

▶ Dot Matrix as the name suggest was made up of little dots and the paper it used had holes down each side for the printer's tractor feed. That was the old days.

▶ Now, printing quality has changed drastically for the best performance.

▶ Ink Jets Printers has some similarities to the Dot matrix printers. The difference is that they have a print head that moves across the paper and creates the image one row of dots at a time.

▶ The goodness of inkjet printers is the inks of different colors can be applied on the paper at the same time, this facilitates it to create full-color images. Most color printers in the homes and offices in now a day are inkjets printers. If you don't possess one as yet, go get yours now. All in one color inkjet printer. You can get it anywhere; Best buy, Circuit City, Brandsmart USA, Wal-Mart, Sam's-club and many other places.

The Famous Laser Printers

I personally call it Famous for its wonders. It is completely different from all the other printers that I mention above. It is extremely economical. It is not often found in the homes, but in the offices. I don't mean it is not in the homes but not in a large quantity.

Fig.10.0

Open tray from here and load papers, then close it by pushing it in.

The thing that makes this machine that good is the Cylinder called a print drum. The drum may also be called a photosensitive drum or a photoreceptor. That drum has a special coating that can hold an electric charge as long as it is in the dark, but loses the charge when touched by light. The Laser light will shine on the drum in just those spots where we want the image to be formed.

Laser Printers use something call Toner instead of Ink and have the capacity to print thousands of documents before the toner finishes. You may consider purchasing one next time but they also cost more than dot matrix and Ink jet printers.

SETTING UP OR INSTALLING YOUR NEW PRINTER

Now you are smart enough to call yourself a technician don't you?

You need to decide where the printer is going to connect, why? Because most printers are presently hybrids. What do you mean by hybrids? I simply mean that they give the user several choices of connections. Serial, Parallel, USB, SCSI, or IEEE 1394 firewire port, and will often have an RJ-45 connector for straight connection to Ethernet. Some printers do have wireless card built in. see figure 10.0 in the above, I have mentioned different connections or ports. Now I am going to focus on the main and simplest one that is "Parallel Port".

▶ The first parallel port (LPT1) is the default printer port in most systems and this the easiest way to install your printer.

▶ Parallel ports also allow faster transfer of data than COM ports. The privilege that one have with a serial connection is that the cable can be longer, up to 50 feet.

▶ Now let's find a proper location for your printer, within 10 feet of your PC. Make sure that you load the tray with paper as in the figure 10.0 from the previous page.

▶ Connect the cable. This is either a round or ribbon cable, usually comes in a 25-pin male D connector (DB-25) on one end and a 25-pin male centronics-style connector on the other. The Centronics connector goes to the printer, and the other end goes to the computer. Like in the figure 10.1

▶ Most of the time your computer system that we call the "BIOS" will quickly recognize the printer and no further set-up will be needed.

This is the USB port

This is the DB-25 Printer port

Fig.10.1

▶ Now it is time to insert the CD that comes with your printer into the CD drive. You are now ready to install the driver for the printer. That CD you insert into the CD-Rom is called "Software" it tells the operating system how to relate to the type of printer that is attached to it. See figure 10.2

▶ Now click on the choice for the driver to be installed and follow the instruction on the screen carefully to finish the installation. See figures 10.3 and 10.4

▶ Notice that when this screen appears, You must click "Yes" or accept in order for the installation to go through. See figure 10.5 and 10.6

▶ Please wait while windows configuring paper port. Preparing setup. Follow the screen until the test page is printed. Figure 10.7

A little about "Serial Port" installation.

There is no big difference when installing to a Serial Port. Just the same as parallel port.

Now the serial standard used by printers and most other serial devices is called RS-232. That could be either 9-pin or 25-pin female connector (DB-9 or DB-25); you will have to read the printer's manual. Some printers will need a cable with certain signals switched rather than going from pin 1 to pin 1 etc.

Make sure to program the printer to accept serial input. Consult the printer manual for this step.

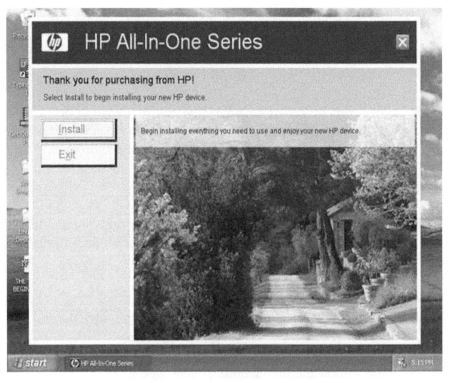

Fig.10.2

Fig.10.3

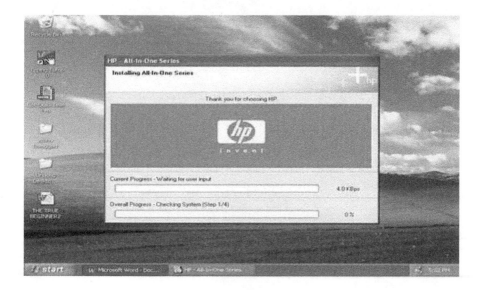

Fig.10.4

Fig.10.5

Fig.10.6

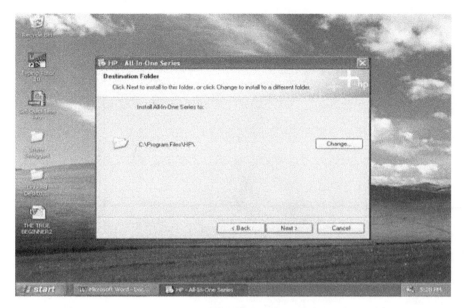

Fig.10.7

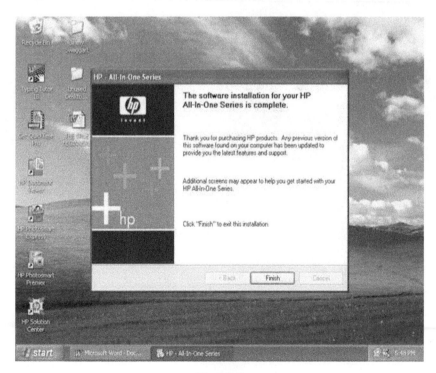

Fig.10.8

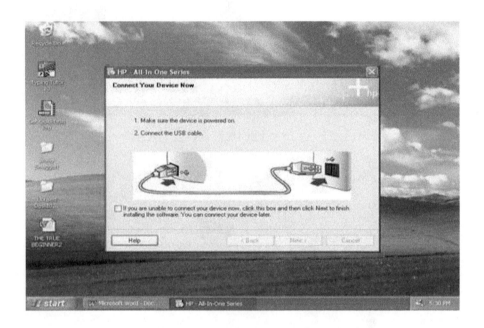

Fig.10.9

The superior man is distressed
By his want of ability.
By Confucius

CHAPTER 7

PLAYING MUSIC ON YOUR PC

This is a very exciting section because Music plays a vital part in human life. Whatever problem you may have by listening to music or if you can play an instrument it will relax your mind.

You can use the CD-ROM drive on your computer to play music, in addition to loading software. Music creates an atmosphere to help you concentrate while you are working.

Whether you are writing a letter, working on a spreadsheet, or painting a picture. Even if you have a sound system, playing CDs on your PC means you can use headphone, in fact will not disturb anyone in the room.

Another plus is that you are using one piece of hardware, thus saving energy. Windows has a built in CD player; all you have to do is load the CD of your choice to hear. Sit back and enjoy.

SOUND AND VISION

Your computer is very useful when playing audio CDs that include multimedia content. These are just like conventional audio CDs that you play on a home stereo system but they contain extra files when you view them with your PC's CD-ROM drive. The content of the files varies, but usually includes information on the instruments played and background notes on the artist. They may even contain music videos. Children especially like the versatility of multimedia. It can be a great way to attract their attention in a subject.

FIND THE CD PLAYER SCREEN

▶ You can find the CD player controls by using the menus or insert a CD into the drive and click Ok on the next screen.

▶ Click on start, gently place the mouse pointer on programs.

▶ Then move the pointer to Windows Media Player and click it once. Then click play that is at bottom left of the player screen. See figure 11.0

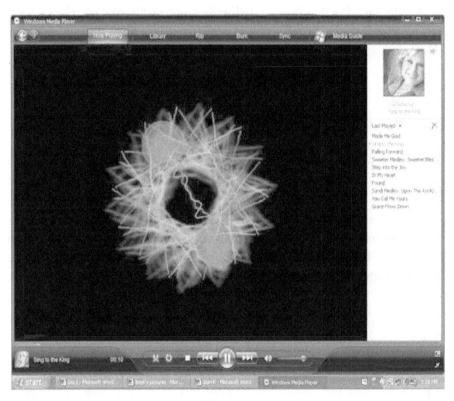

Fig.11.0

▶ Your speakers may have their own volume controls, as well as treble and bass controls. Windows also provides a volume control for your speakers. To open it, simply double-click the speaker icon in the system Tray, next to the clock in the bottom right corner of your screen. If there is no speaker icon in the tray disregard it.

▶ You can click Start, Programs, Accessories, Entertainment then click on Volume Control to access to access it. See figure 11.1

Fig.11.1

▶ Use your mouse pointer to drag the volume control knob up and down to the level that you want it to be.

▶ The next way you can access Volume Control is to go to Start, move the mouse pointer to the word Setting, then drag the pointer to the words Control Panel, and click it once. The Control Panel drop box will appear like the one below. Figure 11.2

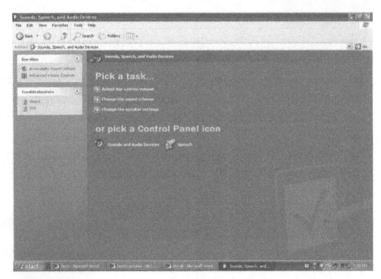

Fig.11.2

▶ Next step click Sounds, Speech, and Audio Devices. Another screen will appear for it. See figure 11.3

▶ Next step click Adjust the System Volume, then Sounds and Audio Devices Properties drop box will appear. See figure 11.4

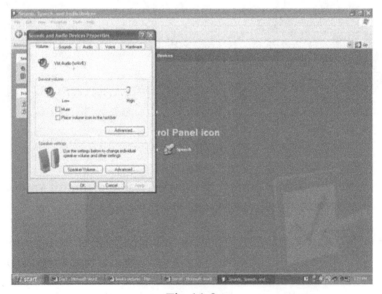

Fig.11.3

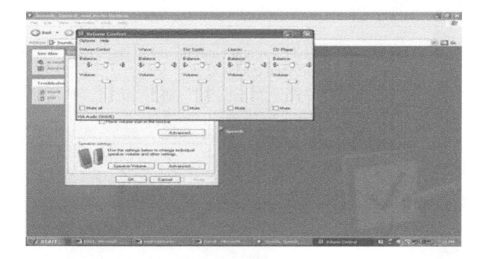

Fig.11.4

▶ To the left is Low and on the right side is High, you can change it by dragging it with your mouse pointer to either side.

▶ You can also retrieve the volume control from the Sounds and Audio Devices Properties by clicking Advanced that is below the sentence Place volume icon in the taskbar. See figure 11.5

▶ Notice sometimes the volume control may be in "Mute" if your system use to play fine suddenly there is no sound. First thing to do is to check the Volume control to see if it has a check mark in any of the boxes.

▶ How can I take it out of the "Mute"?

▶ answer-Gently move the mouse pointer to the box where the check appears, then click on it once. And if the volume needs to be adjusted you can do so by dragging it up or down like in the figure 11.6

▶ Now let's talk a little about Sounds. You can modify the sounds. You can even give it a name of your own and save it in the Sound Scheme. How do you do that?

► answer. Simply click on Audio as in the figure 11.6

► Then click in the blue bar and enter the name you'd like to save it then click *save as* then click Ok.

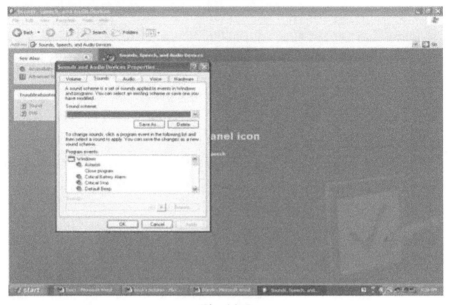

Fig.11.5

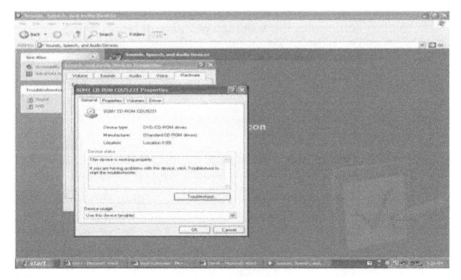

Fig.11.6

▶ If your monitor comes with a built in microphone you will be able to record your voice, make your own CD or DVD as well. As you can see here "Sounds Recording".

▶ Now click voice and click Advance, then click the blue bar where you see Desktop stereo speakers.

▶ Make a selection from the dropping, then click apply then Ok. Also you can click on Performance as it is stated. These settings control how windows play audio. They can help you troubleshoot audio-related problems.

▶ Now let's check Hardware to see what is there for us. As the name suggest hard components that attached to the system and can be communicated with the operating system "OS" or for upgrade. Here in this drop box you are actually look at the sound card that is attached to your device, if you delete anyone of them you may end up with no sound until you restore it from the recycle bin. In this dropping it will state that your hardware is working properly (Enable). If its not working, the word (Disable) will appear. See figure 11.6 of the previous page.

▶ Click Properties, the Creative Audio Properties drop box will appear. Here you can see if the device is working properly or not as in the above picture.

▶ For some reasons sometimes a device does not work because it is disable in the system. You can see Device usage, Use this device {enable} or Do not use this device {disable} the correct sentence you want to see is Use this Device {enable} if there is any more problem click on troubleshoot.

▶ Now click on the word Properties that is beside General.

▶ Here if there is any problem a yellow or a red sign will be placed beside the icon.

▶ Click on driver that is the third and last icon beside Properties. Clicks roll back Driver to restore the previous one. Then click Ok to finish.

▶ Go back to the control Panel, click Sounds, Speech, and Audio Devices, and then click on Speech, as you can see on the note there. You can control the voice properties, see, and other options for text—to-speech translation. Click on Preview Voice did you hear something?

▶ Then, you can also select Audio Output to change the Settings if you are not comfortable with the previous one.

It is a great ability to be able to
Conceal one's ability.
By Larochefoucauld

CHAPTER 8

GETTING ON THE INTERNET

This is the most exciting part for people around the world, with Internet you can be in touch with the world just by a simple click.

▶ Most information you need regardless the area there is no doubt that you will find it.

▶ Your PC (Personal Computer) doesn't have to be the most powerful or up-to-date. You can use it to access the Internet.
You will need a modem to transfer information to and from your computer. You will also need a nearby phone outlet for the modem; but if you are using cable you won't need a phone outlet, which you will learn later.

▶ ISP stands for Internet Service Provider in other words it is a Company that offers a special phone number and often, special software. So after purchasing a computer, you set it at home or in your office. You will need to contact an ISP

▶ What is Software? It is the appropriate name for computer instructions.

▶ These software instructions are organized into sets of instructions called Programs. A software program is a set of instructions to do a particular task. For example, you want to play a game on the computer; you must have a program that contains the instructions for that game. If you want to write a letter, you would use a program for Microsoft word, and for e-mail.

▶ Before I choose an Internet Service Provider. I want to make sure that I have some valuable questions that need to be answered by the company.

► Here is a list of questions you may want to ask:

What is the setup fee for a new Internet account?
What is the monthly subscription charge?
Are there any extra charges after this? Or how long will take before it increases?
Can I connect to the Internet with a local phone call?
What software is provided and what can I use it for?
Do I have to pay an extra charge for it?
Do I have to download the software or are you going to send it to me?
Do I get unlimited usage for a flat fee?
Does it come with full installation instructions?
Is there a support line where I can reach you?
Will the support line help me set up my Internet software?
When is the support line open? Seven days? 24/7 including holidays?
    What connection speeds are available?
Will higher connection speeds be available soon?
What will my e-mail address be like?
Can I have more than one e-mail address so other family members can
    use the account as well? Or will they have separate mailbox?
Do I get any free Web space with this account? How much if any?
What other services are included with the account?

► Once you are not comfortable with the ISP you presently using feel
  free to cancel your account and go to another provider that offers
  better service. However if you want to keep your e-mail address with
  the large web based service such as Hotmail, Yahoo. You can then
  access your e-mail from any ISP and any location using a web browser.

► There are hundreds of Internet service providers out there. MSN,
  AOL, AT&T, EARTH LINK, and COMCAST for fiber optic
  (cable), and many more are out there.

► In now a day's most computers have built in modems inside. There
  are two (2) ways you can view the Device Manager to see if your
  PC has a modem.

► First, use your middle finger on your mouse to right click on the
  "My Computer" icon from your desktop. See figure 11.9

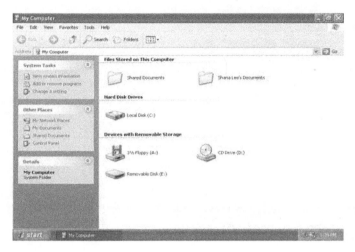

Fig.11.9

▶ Secondly, move your mouse pointer to the word "Manage," and then click it once. A Drop box will appear. See figure 12.0

▶ Thirdly, move the mouse pointer below to the words Device Manager click it once, you will see a list of all the devices for which software is installed on your computer. If you see modem double-click it and the name of a modem will appear. Double-click the name to see a box that tells you if it's working correctly. Does your screen look like the one below? Figure 12.1

Fig.12.0

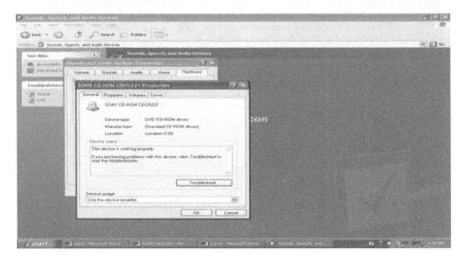

Fig.12.1

▶ To choose the right ISP can be confusing, but it is not that difficult to make your choice. It's important to check whether local call access is available. Some offer specific content, which may or may not be of interest to you. Also 24—hour help or technical support is an extremely import factor.

▶ **WHAT IS "DSL"?**
DSL stands for Digital Subscriber Line. It is connected to Internet Service Provider that uses a standard telephone line but with a specific equipment on each end to create always-on Internet connections at a very high speed that one can hardly notice, especially when compared with analog dial-up connections.

▶ Service levels vary around the United State of America, but the typical upload speed is 384 kilobytes per second (kbps), while download speed comes in at a very nice 2 Megabytes per second (Mbps). One Megabyte equal to 1,000,000 kilobytes
One kilobyte equal to 1,000 bits.

▶ DSL Connection is very easy compare to dial-up and more recent it requires very little setup from a user standpoint. If you have someone that can setup the connection for you there is no need to call a technician but if not a technician will come to your home to install something call Network Interface Card often refer as

(NIC) in the internet-bound Computer and drop off a DSL receiver (often called a DSL modem) see figures 12.2

▶ The receiver connects to the telephone line and the PC. See figures 12.3

▶ The technician (or the user) then configures the TCP/IP (Transmission Control Protocol/ Internet Protocol) protocol options for the Network Interface Card (NIC) to match the settings according to your DSL provider.

▶ Then within a minute you should be able to start surfing the Internet.

▶ Let's look at Cable. It is different compare to DSL. With cable you don't need to have a phone at all. It uses the regular cable TV. Have you ever seen when the lightning strikes, that cable Internet.

▶ Almost every Community in America have cable available. First you have to request it from your cable TV provider then a technician will come with the modem and install the service that you requested it may take up an hour to be completed depending on the tech.

▶ The cable then connected to a modem through something call (NIC) that is Network Interface Card and from the NIC to your Personal Computer (PC) via a UTP (unshielded twisted pair) Ethernet Cable. See figure 12.3 it shows a typical Cable setup.

▶ One of the advantage you have with Cable over DSL is that if you install a TV card in your PC it will serve you as a normal TV. Most cards also come with remote control. Where as DSL doesn't provide this feature. Some how it can save you money. Instead of paying for cable and Internet you only pay for Internet and have both.

▶ Now a little about Wireless technology this is the way to go as the term suggest no wire around your home or office to scare you. It works flawlessly, it create a magical computing experience.

Fig.12.2

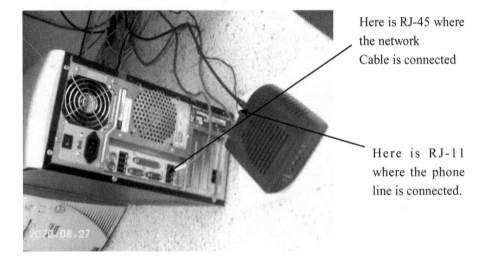

Here is RJ-45 where
the network
Cable is connected

Here is RJ-11
where the phone
line is connected.

Fig.12.3

▶ Most recently you can walk into a fast food like Mc Donald, or a coffee shop, sit down, and open your laptop computer, gets in touch with the world just in a minute without any wire hanging around you.

▶ Just a bit of explanation of how those wireless in those places work. The local Internet café purchases high-speed Internet service from the cable or telecom company, and then connects a wireless access point (WAP) to its network. When you actually go to the place with your laptop PC that is wireless and open a web browser, the NIC in your portable actually communicates with the fully wired DHCP (Dynamic Host Configuration Protocol) server via the WAP as a result you are able to surf the Internet. It appears magical doesn't it?

▶ Now after you have finished having your service installed and running. You can modify the default page for your favorite for example some people prefer MSN.COM instead of YAHOO to be there internet default page so that they can quickly see highlights on the news and other stuff.

▶ Click *start*, then Control Panel, Network and Internet Connections then click Internet Options. Does your screen look like the one below? Figure 12.4

▶ Then type your choice in the box like this; *http://www.yahoo.com* whatever your selection may be that's how to insert it in the box. Then click Apply and then Ok to finish the setup.

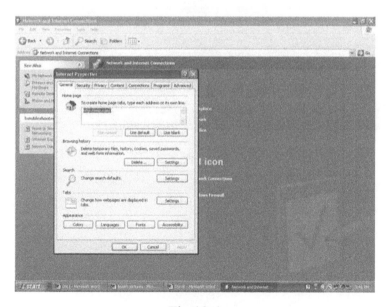

Fig.12.4

▶ Now you are at the desktop screen double-click on Internet explorer sign then the page will open like the one in figures 12.5

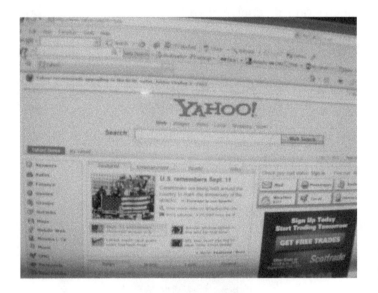

Type your choice here.

Fig.12.5

HOW TO CREATE A FREE E-MAIL ACCOUNT

► It is simple in a minute you will be there. Example, I choose start an Account with Hotmail. First from windows Internet Explorer click on hotmail, then the screen will change like figure 12.6 then click on sign up that is under Windows Live. See figure 12.7

► Now to setup your free e-mail address follow these steps carefully.

► First, click on your choice, you can use hotmail, yahoo or whatever. You can also have more than one e-mail Account. Now let's click on hotmail. Does your screen look like the one below? Figure 12.8

► Click on sign up, then another one will appear like the one on figure 12.9

► Then read the information provided carefully and click on the best package. See figure 13.0

► After you click on your choice another screen will drop like the one in figure 13.1. Insert all the information requested in the entire field.

► Then click I Accept then next

Fig.12.6

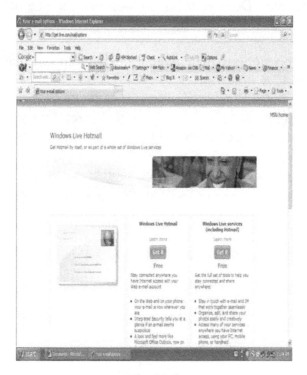

Fig.12.7

Fig.12.8

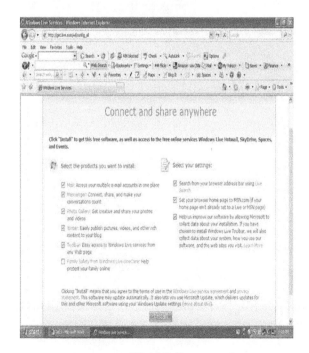

Fig.12.9

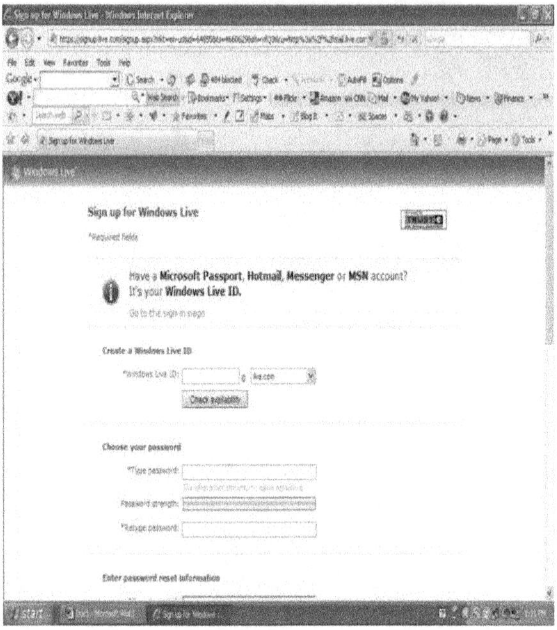

Fig.13.0

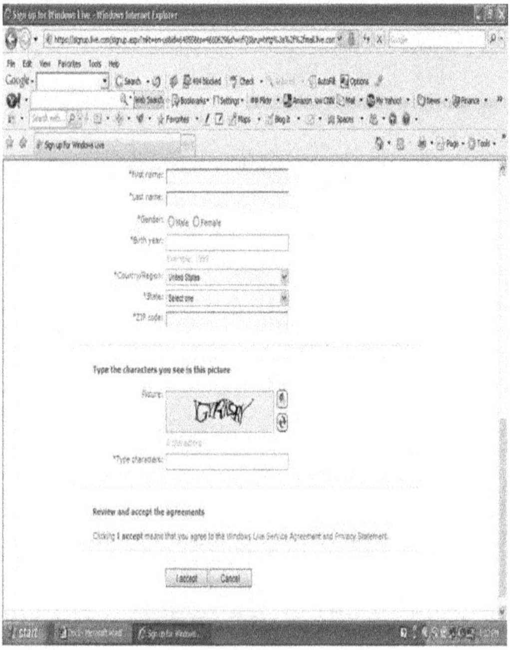

Fig.13.1

VIRUS ISSUES

Make sure that you have an up-to-date Anti-virus program install on your computer even before connecting on the Internet. When you purchase a new computer it always come with a version trial between 30-90 days that puts you in a good shape. No need to be afraid. But do not let the trial version expire. You may end up spending about half of price you paid for the computer to repair it. Prices also vary. Starting from $ 29.99 to $ 179.99. Depending on the shop you go to, and also the features that offer on the software. Some of them are very limited as a result your computer can get infected easily.

▶ Computer virus can be compared like Cancer in human being, that's how hard it is. Same way human suffer with lots of pain same way your PC suffers with pains and aches when it catches a virus. The only prevention is to install good anti-virus software in the system.

▶ As we grow technologically, medically or intellectually, the more HIV cases we have among us regardless of race, language, and ethnic background. How can one solve this deadly disease? Unless using a very strict preventive measure. Don't you agree? Of course I am 100%. It is the same thing with your computer. Do not under estimate it.

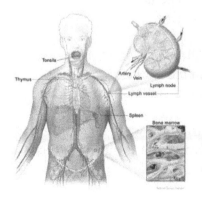

This is an illustration of a selected Virus disease of the Nervous System.

Brain Abscess—Nervous tissue as well as the meninges responds to virus invasion as other tissues do. Phylogenic organisms gaining access to brain tissue produce an inflammatory reaction with pus formation, which results in an abscess. Figure 13.2

Fig.13.2

This is inside of the computer: the brain, heart, and all the other components. Figure 13.3

Fig.13.3

▶ The illustration above is to show you how the viruses creep into your system until it occupies the entire body. That's exactly the way it operates in the computer as well. This is for you to be alert not to spend unnecessarily. You can keep that money into your pocket. See figures 13.2

▶ A good anti-virus program will protect your PC from all of these, and I fully recommend their use on any system, but what good would it serve if you do not have an Internet connection. Almost every week your anti-virus needs to be upgraded, and it will do so on its own as you turn the system on.

▶ I just want to mention a few well-known Anti-viruses for you but there are hundreds of them on the market; McAfee, Norton, Norton Doctor, Symantec, and some Spy ware Protections.

▶ Let's see how to install Anti-virus Software in your system. First open the CD drive as you have learnt earlier, insert the CD properly into the CD-ROM drive and close it, now follow the screen.

▶ Secondly, click on install; follow the instructions on the screen. Remember you must click on "Accept or Agree" to the license agreement in order for the installation to go through. Either on the CD or on the box you will see Product Key, which you need to insert in the box provided on your screen. See figure 13.4 and 13.5

Fig.13.4

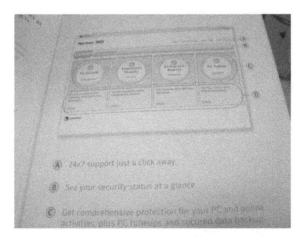

Fig.13.5

▶ As technology advances the more widespread this virus problem will become. They are created by people, especially young men so call clever in computers but not very smart in the way that they should. To learn more about anti-virus go to http//: www.antivirus.com

Intelligence is quickness to apprehend
As distinct from ability, which is capacity
To act wisely on the thing apprehended.
By Alfred N W.

CHAPTER 9

WHAT IS INSIDE MY COMPUTER?

After you are through with this chapter you should be able to know and also identify the different parts of a computer. This chapter is not to teach you how to repair computer. It is merely intended to teach you the part's name.

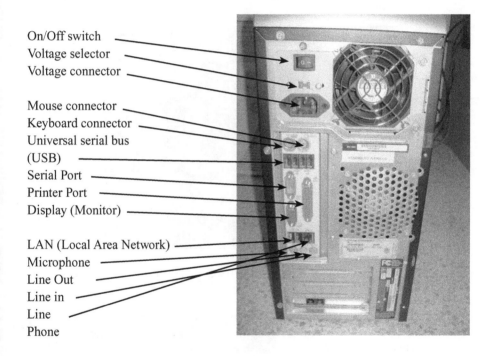

On/Off switch
Voltage selector
Voltage connector

Mouse connector
Keyboard connector
Universal serial bus
(USB)
Serial Port
Printer Port
Display (Monitor)

LAN (Local Area Network)
Microphone
Line Out
Line in
Line
Phone

This shows the rear panel of typical PC showing ports.

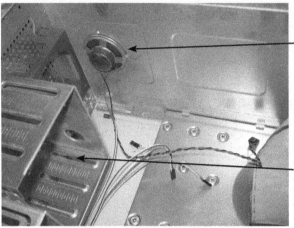

This is inside of the box. It is empty as you can see. Here is an internal speaker

This is the compartment that holds the hard-drive, CD-Rom and Floppy-drive

Power supply and its connectors

This is the back of the Power Supply. Attach the cord here

This is the picture of an ATX Motherboard with a CPU mounted under the cooling fan.

This Athlon CPU (Central Processing Unit)

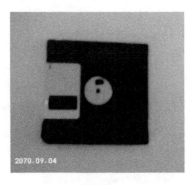

Floppy Disk

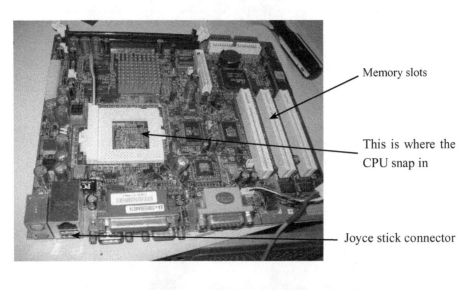

Memory slots

This is where the CPU snap in

Joyce stick connector

This is called RAM (Random Access Memory Module)

Typical modern Floppy Drive

This is a high capacity Hard-Drive
IDE HARD-DRIVE

THIS IS AGP video card

This is a cooling Fan and it is placed at the top of the CPU to keep it cool

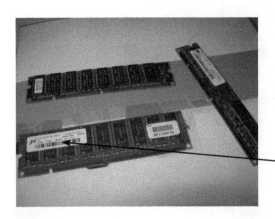

Memories varied in style and size. Here are three Dual Inline Memory Modules.

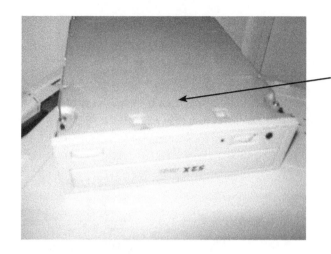

Typical CD-ROM drive

Here is the hole to manually open it.

This is a Modem Card. One hole is for the phone line and the other is for the phone itself to connect

This PCI and ISA video card

This is a Modem with the wires connected to it.
The big black one is the cable, the next small one is the power cord, and the next blue one is the RJ-45
For your Internet

This is a switch. It is a device that allows you to connect more Computer to your Internet

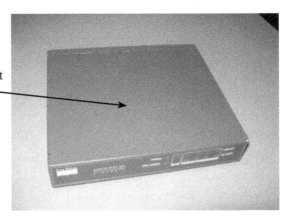

This is showing you the CMOS battery. If your computer cannot keep the right time. This battery needs to change

Mouse

Keyboard

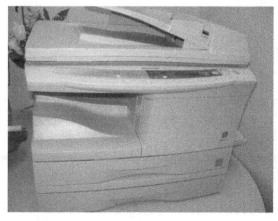

Laser Printer

This is all the parts you have seen so far assemble in one case, attach to the monitor and the printer, which form the computer. It is running perfectly.

This is a Fax Machine

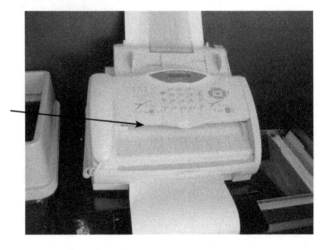

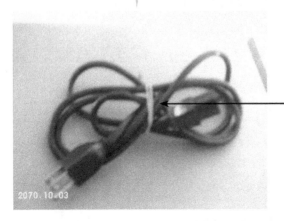

This black wire goes to the back of the computer and the other end to wall or to the surge protector

This off white wire go to the back of the
Display (Monitor) the other end to the wall

This is a Parallel Printer cord ———————→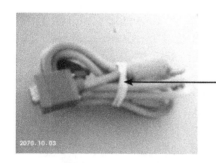

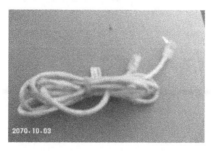

This cable connect to the
Monitor (Display) and the
PC, which is the main box

RJ—45 JACKS

JUST A MOMENT SETTING A GOOD EXAMPLE

It is said that children learn from their elders. Are we aware that example is the best form of TEACHING?

We go about our daily duties seemingly mindless of our responsibilities to those around us, especially the young ones who look for guidelines. The child is told to obey the elders, but when the child acts the way the elder act he is usually punished.

Our actions, our words and language, even our attitudes are very carefully monitored by the younger members of our society. What sort of influence are we having upon such person?

If that is not enough, there are also the newspapers, the TV, Radio and cinema, all exercising their own particular influence and having very deep impressions on young as well as old minds. Do the children stand a chance? Years ago we made use of the expression, as innocent as a child; but is it still valid statement?

It may not be possible or even desirable to dissuade children from getting involved in the numerous spheres that generate negative and vicious vibrations; but it is possible to insure that we lead our lives in a correct and just manner.

If there is honesty and truth in our lives then there is no reason to be ashamed or hide anything we do, not even from our children. If your children love you, they try to be as you are. If we love God, should we attempt to be godly?

As you do, other will follow. Realize your responsibility then carelessness will finish.

www.ingramcontent.com/pod-product-compliance
Lightning Source LLC
Chambersburg PA
CBHW051240050326
40689CB00007B/1004